Wisdom
SPEAKS:
LIFE LESSONS FROM PROVERBS

Dr. Tim Riordan

Wisdom SPEAKS

LIFE LESSONS FROM PROVERBS

Dr. Tim Riordan

GreenTree Publishers
Newnan, GA

Wisdom Speaks: Life Lessons from Proverbs

Printed in the United States of America
ISBN-13: 978-1-944483-21-0 (Greentree Publishers)
ISBN-10: 1-944483-21-7

Follow Dr. Tim Riordan through the following media links:
Website/blog: www.timriordan.me
Twitter: @tim_riordan

Greentree Publishers
www.greentreepublishers.com

DEDICATION

This book is dedicated to my wonderful father, Jerry E. Riordan. You have spoken of wisdom with your words and modeled it with your life. I'm a blessed man to have you as my Dad.

CONTENTS

WOULD YOU LIKE A FREE BOOK?

We are offering the digital version of Book 1 of Dr. Tim Riordan's *Reading the Bible* series as a thank you gift. You will find this to be a useful companion to his other book on Psalms: *Songs from the Heart: Meeting with God in the Psalms.*

This book will not be available for free for long, so visit
www.greentreepublishers.com/free-gift---psalms.html.

Would you be willing to write a brief review?

We would also like to ask up front if you would be so kind as to write a review of this book on Amazon. Reviews will help future readers to be blessed by this helpful resource. You can also learn about other books by this author at the conclusion of the book. We pray you enjoy your study of Proverbs and that God will use this time to enrich your life and spiritual journey.

GreenTree Publishers

Acknowledgements

Writing a book is a consuming yet rewarding project, but it is not a venture one can take alone. First, I am forever grateful to my patient and supportive wife, Sandra. We celebrate 35 blessed years of marriage this year, and I am a fortunate man indeed. My assistant June Black has been an invaluable part of this project with editing and suggestions. I am grateful to have you on my team. I couldn't have completed this project without you.

A number of dear friends and church members read this manuscript at various times, and for those of you who sacrificed your time and opinions, thank you.

Other than my assistant's editorial work and the input of a number of other readers, I am also grateful to my final editor, Adele Brinkley, for her sacrifice and time. Adele, you told me about 25 years ago that you wanted to be my editor, and I'm grateful that you've been with me every step of the way.

Finally, I'd like to thank the wonderful members of the SonRise Baptist Church in Newnan, Georgia. It is my privilege to serve as your pastor. You continuously show your support and love. I am so blessed to call you my church and my friends.

Tim Riordan
May, 2018

CHAPTER ONE
Finding My Way

We stood frozen, clueless as to the path's direction. There was a path. The only problem was that we couldn't see it.

My brother, Dan, and I had planned a backpacking trip on the Appalachian Trail through the Smoky Mountains for more than a year, but we were not prepared for what met us when we topped the approach trail that came up the mountain from Cades Cove: snow. A lot of snow! Above our thighs kind of snow. In retrospect, February is probably not the best time of year to make a trek through the Smokies unless you're a polar bear.

We enjoyed the challenge of hiking through the snow for a few minutes, and then, reality set in. We were in trouble. We had planned to hike twelve to fifteen miles per day, but now, we would do good to make five or six. Our feet were wet and felt like blocks of ice attached to the bottom of our legs. Freezing the tent stakes into the snow with water was necessary to keep the tent from sliding down the mountain.

A few hours of hiking into our second day revealed our greatest challenge: we couldn't see the trail. In many cases on the Appalachian Trail, the direction of the path is obvious, but other times, you are dependent upon seeing the beaten down brush and the eventual marker on a tree in order to make progress toward your goal.

Imagine going across the top of a bald mountain with one to two feet of snow between the bottom of your feet and the actual path. We lost our direction many times, and eventually experienced being frozen in our tracks. We weren't frozen because of the temperature, though it was well below freezing. No, we were frozen because we were clueless about which way to go.

The answer came in one of the most unlikely ways you can imagine. We noticed the tracks of an animal. It looked like possibly a large bobcat or a cougar, which seemed to have been in the same predicament we were now in, except there was nothing frozen about this wild animal. The wild cat had plodded right through the snow, over the ridges, and hadn't thought twice about not seeing the trail markers.

> "Watch the path of your feet, and all your ways will be established."
> Proverbs 4:26

Dan and I decided that since the tracks were going in the right direction, we should just follow them. It made sense to us that an animal who passed this way often would probably use the familiar path, which we hoped was the hiker's trail. We figured we would eventually find a trail marker to confirm that we were heading in the right direction, or we would interrupt a little family time at this big cat's den. Hopefully, it would not be the latter.

The good news is that the creature was smart and served as a perfect guide for us. A little while later, we discovered a marker on a tree indicating that we were going in the right direction.

Finding the Path

Have you ever had a similar experience in your life when you had lost your way and had no idea which way to go to get back on track? It may not have happened on a mountain trail in the dead of winter, but it could have happened while navigating the challenges of marriage or in parenting a teenager. It's possible you encountered the *frozen in your tracks* scenario when trying to work your way out of a financial crisis or in dealing with an unsolvable problem at your office. What do you do when there's no trail markers to tell you which way to go?

The writer of Proverbs used the imagery of walking on a path to describe making forward progress in life. For example, consider the words of one of the most familiar passages in Proverbs:

> *Trust in the Lord with all your heart*
> *And do not lean on your own understanding.*
> *In all your ways acknowledge Him,*
> *And He will make your paths straight.*
> —Proverbs 3:5-6

As a backpacker, I find it interesting that God said He would make our paths straight but not level. Life is not easy. I've often drawn parallels between climbing a mountain and living my life. Sometimes, it takes a lot of blood, sweat, and tears, but the view from the top is always breathtaking and brings glory to my Creator.

God reveals to us today through the Proverbs that life is all about choices, and He gave us this book of wisdom as a guide to help us stay on the right path. Very much like our wildcat friend in the Smoky Mountains, whom I'm glad we never met, Proverbs can help us navigate the uncertainties and challenges of this journey we call life. By following God's wisdom, we can stay on the path and experience God's blessings in our lives.

The Format of Proverbs

When I mention to people that I am writing a book on Proverbs or that I plan to teach through the book during the summer, I typically hear the same response: "Oh, I love Proverbs." When I ask, "What is your favorite?" I typically get blank stares and a lot of throat clearing.

One reason that we have a hard time holding these wonderful nuggets of wisdom in our minds is because the individual proverbs seem to be like multi-colored gems scattered around a field. We know each gem has value, but it seems difficult to order the gems in our minds and thereby provide a means by which we can hold these truths in our memories.

My hope is that *Wisdom Speaks* can be a resource to help all of us understand this awesome biblical book of Proverbs and learn how to mine the gems of truth in a such a way that we will never be frozen in our tracks again. Life is not just about paths; it's also about crossroads. We often stand at forks in the road of life struggling with which direction we should take. Sometimes, the proper path should seem obvious, but life is filled with competing influences. Some of the voices we hear are quite loud, but the words we should listen to may very well be a whisper.

> *"Listen to my instruction and be wise; do not ignore it" (NIV).*
> Proverbs 8:33

Although at first glance, much of the Proverbs seems to be as disconnected as the pieces of a jigsaw puzzle that were accidentally dropped on the floor, you will discover that these wonderful tidbits of truth offer amazing continuity. Though many of the proverbs stand alone with no apparent connection to the previous statement of wisdom, Proverbs may not be as "hodge podge" as you may have once thought.

In an effort to understand better this important Bible book, we need to consider several things. First, we need to look briefly at the unique genre of wisdom writing. We will find some parallel attributes with other books in this genre that will help us to get a better grasp on this book. Next, we'll answer the normal questions of who the human author was and when the book was written. We'll try to ascertain the writer's motives, other than being inspired by God, and seek to gain an understanding of who first read this treasure trove of practical advice. Some of these issues will be addressed in a companion book that is part of my *Reading the Bible* series called *Reading Proverbs* (available summer 2018). *Wisdom Speaks* is intentionally less technical and will hopefully guide you straight into the Proverbs without as much preliminary work, though I will still cover some foundational material in the next chapter. I do encourage you, however, to take the time to dig a little deeper.

When I do a Bible book study, I always look for patterns and try to divide the book into sections. Proverbs can be outlined, but we will discover that the outline is both linear and nonlinear. You have probably already discovered sections of Proverbs that flow from verse to verse while other sections make you feel more like you're on a pogo stick jumping from one detached truth to the next.

We will search for common themes and organize the individual proverbs by topic. We need to keep in mind that Proverbs was not originally written as a book. Proverbs were short statements offered to provide wisdom and direction for life, and they were often written as stand-alone morsels that were later compiled.

You will discover that *Wisdom Speaks* can be viewed as if it were written in two parts. Part 1 consists of six chapters. The first two are more foundational in nature, and chapters three through six move into biblical teaching of some of the scriptures that help us to understand the overall theme and purpose of Proverbs.

In the second part of the book, beginning with chapter seven, I begin looking at some of the topics presented in Proverbs. I will pull out various proverbs that relate to a particular topic, and we will consider God's teaching on the issue. You will notice that at the end of each chapter, I share some questions and comments for personal thought. You could use these in a discussion setting with a small group of Christians.

The intent of *Wisdom Speaks* is to guide you through a devotional study of a number of the proverbs in order to encourage you and help you find answers to life's complexities. You may want to read this book as a daily devotional or study it with your small group. It is my hope that the life-changing truths of the book of Proverbs will be for you greater than simply tracks in the snow but rather life-altering, unerring truths that will indeed be a guide for your life.

FURTHER THOUGHT

- Have you ever found yourself "frozen" because you didn't know which way to go? What do you typically do when you find yourself confused about the direction of your next step?
- Go back to page 3 and read Proverbs 3:5-6. Have you ever "leaned on your own understanding?" What typically happens?

- Have you ever read Proverbs before? Do the topics seem jumbled or disjunct to you? Think back to any of the Proverbs you have read. What are some topics you remember being covered?

- How to you plan to read *Wisdom Speaks*? Will it be as a devotional or as a Bible study? Do you plan to read it alone or in a group? Write out a statement of what you hope to learn from your study of Proverbs.

CHAPTER TWO
The Foundation of Proverbs

Foundations are critical to the strength of a building. When we're house shopping, however, we don't usually take pictures of the foundation. They are best unnoticed, but their importance cannot be overlooked. In this chapter, we'll dive a little deeper into some of the more technical aspects of studying Proverbs in order to gain a better understanding of the supporting structure of Proverbs.

Who Wrote Proverbs?

The book of Proverbs is set in Israel during King Solomon's reign. Although Solomon was not the only contributor to Proverbs, he wrote the majority of the book. Other authors God used to write this book include unnamed sages (22-24), Agur (30), and Lemuel (31), but we often think of this book as the proverbs of Solomon because he contributed the most to this collection. It is important to note that God inspired these writers to share these thoughts because He wanted them included in His Word for us.

Although we know when Solomon lived and have a general time period in mind for the date of the book of Proverbs, it is significant that the book itself does not give us a time context nor an original audience. In a sense, this omission helps to present the timelessness of this writing.

Of course, we know that all of the Word of God is true and relevant for our day, but it is clear that the wisdom of Proverbs is timeless.

Understanding Style

Proverbs is the third of three books of poetry from the Old Testament (Job, Psalms, and Proverbs), and it falls into the larger category of wisdom writings. If you want to read additional thoughts on Hebrew poetry, I wrote a chapter on the subject in my book, *Reading Psalms*, and you will also discover a number of other helpful resources on the subject.

Because Proverbs is Hebrew poetry, you will find some similarities to other poetic passages, such as Psalms. A large portion of Proverbs consists of couplets, or two statements, that fall into one of several categories, including contrasting couplets, synonymous couplets, or a style I'll just call a continuous couplet as it continues the thought in the second phrase that is presented in the first phrase.

Understanding style will enhance your reading of Proverbs. As you read through this book of wisdom, take note of the style of a particular proverb and consider the significance of the type of couplet used and how that impacts the meaning of the verse.

Consider the Big Picture

At first glance, Proverbs may seem to be a jumbled-up collection of wise sayings, but with study, you will see distinct divisions in the book and a unification of these divisions. These divisions are typically created based upon authorship. While commentators use various terms to describe the divisions, the division marks are fairly succinct. Consider this outline:

1. Introduction and Statement of Purpose - 1:1-7
2. The Pursuit of Wisdom - 1:8-9:18
3. The Proverbs of Solomon - 10:1-22:18
4. The Proverbs of the Wise - 22:17-24
5. Hezekiah's Collection of Solomon's Proverbs - 25-29
6. The Words of Agur - 30
7. The Words of Lemuel - 31

Keep in mind that while a particular author wrote a section of the book of Proverbs, this author did not sit down to write the whole section as a unit. Proverbs were typically written one statement at a time. You will find that chapters one through nine are written in a more cohesive fashion and were intended to be read as a larger collection of sayings, but the individual proverbs in much of the rest of the book were probably penned one at a time as memorable statements of truth.

Having this understanding will impact the way you read the book of Proverbs. You can read each section as a collection of a certain author, and that approach will certainly offer value. You may also want to consider the individual proverbs and choose those that are most applicable to commit to memory or print on a placard.

While the divisions of Proverbs are obvious and distinct, the topics and themes of the book are manifold. The main theme of the book is that wisdom comes from God and that applying wisdom to daily living is our choice and God-given responsibility. We have looked at the *what* and the *who*. The book of Proverbs begins in the first chapter by presenting the *why*.

Why Was Proverbs Written?

If we are going to understand the message of Proverbs, we need to know why these proverbs were written and collected. The opening verses answer this question for us.

> *To know wisdom and instruction,*
> *To discern the sayings of understanding,*
> *To receive instruction in wise behavior,*
> *righteousness, justice and equity;*
> *To give prudence to the naive,*
> *To the youth knowledge and discretion.*
> —Proverbs 1:2-4

To Help Us to Know Wisdom

The theme or purpose of Proverbs is communicated with a few focal words, with the most prominent word being *wisdom*. Solomon began his statement of purpose with these words, "To know wisdom and instruction." The word translated as *wisdom* comes from a Hebrew word that means "skill or expertise in living."[1] Accomplishing anything of significance requires skill, and God wants us to be skilled at life.

Notice that Solomon's goal was that his readers might *know* wisdom. As important as the word *wisdom* is to our understanding of Proverbs, the word *know* may be equally as important. This word comes from the Hebrew word *yadah*. While we translate it as *to know*, the Hebrew word emphasizes an intimate acquaintance with something; a personal relationship is implied.

Consider how *yadah* as used in Genesis 4:1 "And Adam knew Eve his wife; and she conceived." The Psalmist called us to worship with these words from God in Psalm 46:10, "Cease striving and know that I am God." Whether the context is the relationship between a man and his wife or the experience of a worshipper relating to God, the Jewish people believed that knowledge was gained through experience. Think about the implications of this word as Solomon communicated the purpose for writing Proverbs. God wants us to embrace this practical knowledge about life. Wisdom is not meant as factual data to be added to our memory banks, but rather it is to be experienced in the trenches of life as we put it to practice.

To Offer Us Instruction for Daily Living

Wisdom is not the only benefit to be gleaned from this inspired book. In the same breath with wisdom, Solomon stated that he also wanted his readers to experience *instruction*, or as some translations render it, *discipline*. This particular word refers to the process of moral education.

It points to correcting behavior that is wrong and setting a person on the right path for success in life. The under-lying message of this word is that your character influences everything about your life. Billy Graham once said, "When wealth is lost, nothing is lost; when health is lost, something is lost; when character is lost, all is lost." One of the key messages of this book is that God wants us first to be a person of character. In other words, be the right person before you do the right thing. Our actions will always be an overflow of our character.

> "A good name is to be more desired than great wealth, favor is better than silver and gold."
>
> Proverbs 22:1

Not only does the Hebrew word that is translated *instruction* carry with it the idea of moral instruction, but it also conveys the concept of discipline. There is a sense in which this idea points to correcting someone who is going in the wrong direction. We humans are like water: we always run in the direction of least resistance, meaning our natural tendency is to go in the wrong direction. Doing the right thing and making the wisest decisions will always meet resistance. For this reason, Jesus said, "The way is narrow that leads to life, and there are few who find it" (Matthew 7:14). Proverbs 14:12 states, "There is a way which seems right to a man, but its end is the way of death."

Think for a moment about your life. I can't imagine anyone not wanting to be on the right path for success in life. Are you traveling that path right now and experiencing success in your life? Do you have skill or expertise in living? The book of Proverbs is written for you and me. God wants us to choose the right path that honors Him and blesses us.

To Help Us Develop Sound Discipline

Another important theme in Proverbs is *discipline*. I can't think of another word more important (other than Jesus) that our society needs today. We lack discipline in every area of our lives: financial, physical, emotional, mental, and spiritual. Proverbs 12:1 states, "Whoever loves discipline loves knowledge, but he who hates reproof is stupid." The focus of this theme is upon moral discipline, and it points to training and correction. Consistently choosing the right path in life requires training the mind and the heart. It necessitates correction along the way for we sometimes make poor choices resulting in potentially disastrous consequences. This Bible book is provided to us, in part, as a tool for personal discipline.

I quoted another important word in the book of Proverbs in the first verse of chapter twelve: *stupid*. In my home growing up, saying the word *stupid* was akin to cursing. If Proverbs 12:1 had been read in church when I was a young boy, I would have been stunned. Now, however, I know that the word simply means lacking sense or understanding. It points to the fool who ignores wise teaching. Though the Hebrew word is different, being *stupid* relates to being a *fool*. According to Proverbs

1:7, "Fools despise wisdom and instruction." One objective of Proverbs is to keep us from being foolish.

Additional Key Concepts

Solomon wrote with a *naïve* person in mind. You'll quickly see that Proverbs appears to be written to a young man. This boy is naive or simple, meaning this young man is untaught. It is not necessarily saying that he is a fool, at least not yet. The description means that he has not had the opportunity in life to learn some of the important lessons that lead to success. Proverbs is offered to the naïve as a guide that will help us gain wisdom for daily living.

You will see the theme of the *fear of the Lord* (1:7) repeated throughout Proverbs. Although we need to have a healthy fear of God (I'll address this concept in the next chapter), the meaning of this phrase points to revering God by honoring and respecting Him. Fearing God is a key theme of Proverbs and foundational to gaining wisdom.

I mentioned the word *success* earlier, and we must be careful to define this term from God's perspective. From a biblical view, success has more to do with who you are becoming than with what you have accomplished. In our culture, we typically tie

> "Commit your works to the Lord and your plans will be established."
>
> Proverbs 16:3

success to finances and accomplishments. God, however, connects success to obedience and character. God is more focused on us growing in Christ-likeness and using our gifts and talents effectively for His purposes. As you read through the book of Proverbs, you will see a theme of success running through the book. While growing our businesses and our financial base has value, God is most concerned that *we* are growing and blessing people around us. You will find a lot of emphasis in Proverbs on our relationships with other people more so than on our accumulation of things.

According to Tremper Longman, one word that is often translated as *successful* also means *to have insight*.[2] Our success depends upon us viewing ourselves, other people, and our circumstances properly with deep *insight*. I pray that as you read through this wonderful book of wisdom that God has included in His word that you will find great success in your life.

FURTHER THOUGHT

- Have you ever thought about Proverbs as being a collection of individual proverbs? Why do you think we typically attribute the book to Solomon?

- On page 10, I mentioned three different types of couplets used in Proverbs. Take just a moment to scan through Proverbs to see if you can find an example of each of these three types.

- If someone asked you why Proverbs was written, other than the fact that God wanted it to be written, what would you say?

- In this chapter, I mentioned a few key words or concepts covered in Proverbs. Write down those words in the space below and watch for these words to pop up in your reading.

- How would you define *success* from God's perspective? Take just a few moments to ask God if He will help you to experience success as you read through Proverbs.

CHAPTER THREE
What Are You Afraid Of?

I am typically not a fearful person. I've climbed cliffs, dove off waterfalls, went scuba diving with sharks, and took advanced geometry in ninth grade. I do have a horrible fear, however. I'm not afraid of snakes, sharks, spiders, or hornets. I've never been sky diving, though I'm willing to go. I am, however, petrified of rats. I've had some run ins with the little vermin that make my skin crawl, and I have had a hard time getting over my fear. If I have to go into a shed at night where one of these creatures from the pit might be hiding, I wake up the little demon by hitting the sides of the building with a stick and pray that if one is present, it will run away before I enter the structure.

I know that I shouldn't be afraid of rats. It's actually silly to be afraid of these detestable, parasite ridden, bubonic plague carrying fiends. The typical rat weighs less than a pound, and I weigh…well, let's just say that I'm bigger than they are by a lot. I'd still rather face a heard of wild boar than be cornered by one rat.

Is Fear Good?

My fear of rats is unfounded and unreasonable. How about you? Are you afraid of anything? If you are, don't fret. Fear is not necessarily a bad thing if it's the right kind

of fear. It must be good, because Proverbs 24:18 begins
with these words, *"How blessed is the man who fears always."*
That verse feels wrong because there are so many other
verses in the Scripture that tell us not to be afraid, but the
Scripture is never wrong. I think the problem has to do
with our understanding of the word *fear*. While God calls
us to put our confidence and trust in Him and not be
afraid, there is a healthy kind of fear that should consume
our lives daily.

In Solomon's opening words to this collection of
proverbs, he sets up the themes of the book and calls his
readers to pursue wisdom and
knowledge. In Proverbs 1:7, God
directed Solomon to draw a line in
the sand to indicate the starting
point to a life of wisdom: "The fear
of the Lord is the beginning of
knowledge; fools despise wisdom
and instruction." With just a few

> "If you have
> knowledge, let
> others light their
> candles at it."
>
> Thomas Fuller

simple words, God is directing us to the starting line to
the race for wisdom and knowledge. From reading the
whole book of Proverbs, you will realize that this race is a
marathon and not a sprint.

When Solomon said that some-thing is *the beginning of
knowledge*, he pointed to the process of obtaining wisdom
or to the journey toward knowledge. It is a process—a
life-long process.

It amuses me up to think back to my late teens or early
twenties. I was so smart then, or maybe I should say I

thought I was so smart. It's amazing how ignorant I became with age. I eventually learned that I wasn't all that smart after all. Wisdom is not something obtained because you've read a few books or received a degree or two. It is a journey that has a starting point and a destination. So, what is the starting point? Where does this race begin? It begins with *the fear of the Lord.*

One problem I have with this verse is that I connect *the fear of the Lord* with the fear of rats. They're not the same. The Hebrew word that is translated as fear in Proverbs 1:7 can mean terror, but it means so much more.

Are You Afraid of God?

Before we focus on what this verse means, I need to speak briefly to a healthy fear of God. Just as it's improper for a child to be scared to death of his father, it would be wrong for us to shake with dread in God's presence. However, we have walked away from the time where our society viewed God as someone to be feared. I don't suggest we cower before God as if we were bowing before the great and terrible Oz, but at the same time, we should recognize God's power and separation from humanity. When was the last time we fell on our faces before God and said, "Woe is me for I am ruined" (Isa. 6:5) or even entertained the thought that God is still a *consuming fire* Heb. 12:29)?

I remember a Christian band coming to sing for my youth group when I was a young teenager. They sang a song that included the lyrics, "Jesus is my buddy, and I'm a buddy to Him." I get what the song writer was trying to convey, but I don't find people in the Scripture speaking of God with such flippant language. As I look around at our society today, we may need a good dose of trembling fear at the feet of God.

Moses was in the unique spot that allowed him to see God—at least His back. If you know the story of Exodus 33, you know that Moses asked to see God's glory. God replied in verse twenty, *"You cannot see My face, for no man can see Me and live!"* God allowed Moses, however, to view His back. I realize that God was revealing Himself to Moses in human terms. He is not limited to a face, a front, or a back, but nevertheless, He allowed Moses to see some aspect of His being.

God and Moses were quite close; however, Moses would never call God his buddy. When Moses first erected the tabernacle in the wilderness, God visited Israel in a powerful, unforgettable way. Moses didn't give God a high five. Instead, God's glory filled the tabernacle, and Moses was unable to even enter the tent. After God instructed Moses about the sacrificial system, God said this to him in Leviticus 22:2, *"Tell Aaron and his sons to be careful with the holy gifts of the sons of Israel, which they dedicate to Me, so as not to profane My holy name; I am the Lord."* We probably need to give more thought about being *careful* and not *profaning* God's holy name.

While the scripture, especially the Old Testament, speaks of God's separation from humanity because of His holiness, we are also quite aware that God reached across the chasm that separates us from Him through Jesus. While God's holiness leads us to fear Him from a distance, His grace calls us to love Him up close. I am grateful that Jesus called His followers His friends. I think balance is an important principle in any relationship.

A Healthy Dose of Fear

We need to understand the role of fear in our relationship with God. Solomon said that the fear of God is the beginning of wisdom. This word *fear* not only means to tremble in dread before something, but it can also mean to respect or revere something or someone. In Proverbs, we will see that it is essential that we have an understanding of the holiness and the majesty of God that makes Him our Sovereign, and we will also discover that fearing God points to our need for an attitude of respect and reverence.

If we do not have this attitude of reverence and respect of God and His position as the supreme authority of our lives, we will never take the first step in the journey of wisdom. *The fear of the Lord is the beginning of wisdom.* Remember that wisdom is a journey and not a destination, but the journey begins with an attitude of reverence before a holy God who is not only a consuming fire but also a friend who sticks closer than a brother (Pr. 18:24).

Reverencing God means not only mentally acknowledging His divine attributes, but also willfully surrendering to His sovereign rule over our lives. God's sovereignty requires submission. I used to hear preachers

say, "God is either Lord of all or He is not Lord at all."
Fearing God means that we understand His place as the
King of the universe and the Ruler of our hearts. If we do
not submit to His rule, then we do not fear Him.

This motto verse says that the fear of God is *the
beginning of wisdom*. I've mentioned already that this idea
points to the process aspect of our journey of wisdom, but
I want us to pause on this phrase for just a moment. As
you read through Proverbs, you quickly see that God is
offering guidance on many areas of life including laziness,
love and friendship, parenting, business partnerships,
marriage, money, and our spiritual lives, to name a few.
Although we can quickly connect spiritual counsel to this
call for godly wisdom, is it just as easy to put our work
ethic in the same spiritual basket? Yes! A thousand times
YES!

We must understand that we
do not just do spiritual things. We
are spiritual beings. We do not
have a compartment in our lives
entitled religion or spiritual. If we
are Christians, EVERYTHING
about our lives is spiritual. Our

> *"There's no such thing as compart-mental spirituality for we are spiritual beings."*

society has created compartmental living, so we have
relegated our spiritual life to an activity on Sunday
mornings. If we are really spiritual, we oftentimes think,
we extend our spirituality to small group studies, Wednes-
day night discipleship, or even a daily quiet time. In our
minds, these activities mean that really spiritual people

have a bigger spiritual file than marginally spiritual people because they add a few more religious events to their packed week's agenda.

Notice how Solomon says that the fear of the Lord is the beginning of wisdom. He doesn't say that fearing God is the beginning of spiritual wisdom or religious practices. Because wisdom encompasses every area of life, fearing God is essential to life. This idea spiritualizes everything about our lives. It means that we do not have a spiritual compartment and a secular compartment but rather everything we do is spiritual.

This truth is why the Apostle Paul was later inspired to write, "*Whether, then, you eat or drink or whatever you do, do all to the glory of God*" (1 Cor 10:31). If we are going to apply wisdom to our lives as employees, then being a good employee starts with fearing the Lord. If we're going to apply wisdom to parenting and marriage, then being a good spouse and parent begins with knowing God.

Consequences of not Fearing God

Fearing the Lord is an important aspect of finding success in life, but what if a person decides he will not fear the Lord? This person should first of all consider the fact that choosing not to stand rightly before God through repentance and faith in Jesus means that he is making an eternal decision that affects everything in his life. Fearing the Lord is not just the first step of wisdom, but it is the first step of salvation. You cannot be a Christian without fearing God. If you choose not to fear God, you are

choosing your own destiny apart from Him. The Bible
says that destiny is hell. Consider Jesus' words recorded in
Matthew 7:13-14, "*Enter through the narrow gate; for the gate is
wide and the way is broad that leads to destruction, and there are
many who enter through it. For the gate is small and the way is
narrow that leads to life, and there are few who find it.*" The
narrow gate is the *fearing God* gate. It is the way to life, and
Jesus stated that there is only one way to life: Him. Jesus
said in John 14:6, "*I am the way, and the truth, and the life; no
one comes to the Father but through me.*"

Some people scoff at the notion of eternal damnation.
Some people consider the words of Jesus to be nothing
more than self-aggrandizement. Others consider Christianity to be a crutch for the weak, while still others think
of it as something they will eventually get around to.

> "Nothing gives rest
> but the sincere
> search for truth."
>
> Blaise Pascal

Many years ago, French phi-
losopher and scientist Blaise
Pascal presented a challenge that
has become known as Pascal's
Wager. He said that reason alone
cannot prove conclusively that
God and immortality exists.
After considering all of the evidence for Christianity, you
are still called upon to make a choice—hence a wager.
You have only two choices: either God is or He is not.
Pascal presented two possible conclusions. If you accept
that God is, and you win, you win everything. If you lose,
you lose nothing. If you reject God and win, you win

nothing. If you lose, you lose everything. The choice is yours to make.

Proverbs 1:7 points to an additional consequence we will experience if we choose not to fear God. Look at the couplet again:

The fear of the Lord is the beginning of knowledge;
   Fools despise wisdom and instruction.

The first line focuses on the positive consequence of fearing the Lord: the beginning of knowledge. The second phrase presents the consequence of not fearing the Lord by referring to this type of person as a fool. The word translated as *fool* comes from a word that means *to thicken*. The idea is describing someone who is thick headed or even stupid. Solomon said that the consequence of being a fool is despising wisdom and instruction. To despise something is to hate it or show contempt for it. If people despise wisdom and instruction, they will end up on a path to destruction and failure because they will go in the opposite direction of success.

What are you afraid of? I hope that after reading Proverbs 1:7, you are afraid of God. I hope that fear is not one of trembling dread like a child may have before an abusive father. I hope your fear is reverence and respect as you recognize the God you serve is love and the Sovereign of the universe.

- Do you have any fears? If so, what?
- What do you think Solomon meant when he said fear of the Lord is the beginning of knowledge?
- Do you feel tension between fearing God and loving God? How do you reconcile the two?
- Imagine wisdom as a journey and the beginning point is fearing God. If this journey were represented as a continuum, where would you place yourself and why?

⟶

- How do you respond to someone who says Christianity is only a crutch for the weak?
- What is your definition of a fool?

CHAPTER FOUR
Wisdom's Cry

On Sunday morning, April 14, 1912, passengers aboard the RMS Titanic were supposed to have participated in a lifeboat drill, but for some reason, the drill was canceled. Maybe they thought they could do it on Monday morning, but for many passengers, Monday morning never came. Another amazing fact about the sinking of the Titanic that baffles a lot of people is that ship operators aboard the ill-fated vessel received numerous warnings about icebergs, but these warnings were largely ignored.

Ignored warnings are not that uncommon. We can probably all think of a few. Seven years before the horrific Indian Ocean tsunami in 2004 that killed more than 230,000 people, a top government official in Thailand warned of a coming disaster. He was called "crazy" and banned from some parts of Thailand because his presence was bad for tourism. On January 27, 1986, Morton Thiokol engineer, Allan MacDonald, refused to sign off on the launch recommendation for the Space Shuttle Challenger stating that the shuttle was unsafe. The next day, the mission was not aborted, and 73 seconds into the flight, the Challenger exploded.

Ignorance is Bliss – Really?

We all shake our heads at these stories and wonder how such warnings could be ignored, but we are often guilty of ignoring warnings. Proverbs 1:20-22 contains a warning that is often overlooked, but we ignore at our own peril. Consider King Solomon's inspired words:

Wisdom shouts in the street,
   She lifts her voice in the square;
At the head of the noisy streets she cries out;
   At the entrance of the gates in the city she utters her sayings:
How long, O naive ones, will you love being simple-minded?
   And scoffers delight themselves in scoffing and fools hate knowledge?

Wisdom is personified in this passage as a woman shouting for attention and waving the warning flag. She faces some obstacles to her warning, however. The streets were noisy with people hurrying about their business. The people were naive and not interested in her wise guidance. And many people surrounding her were scoffers and fools. The noisy streets, simple-minded people, and scoffers are not problems encountered only by Lady Wisdom, but they are also typical challenges we encounter every day. I have pictured the noisy streets as the busyness of our own lives and society. Everyone is preoccupied with crazy schedules, deadlines, and "to do lists" that are largely unchecked. My life is often one big noisy street, and I can easily turn a deaf ear to the warnings of Lady Wisdom. So can you.

Being simple-minded is another problem we all face when it comes to acting rightly in the midst of life's complexities. This passage uses two synonyms for the same concept. God refers to the *naive ones* and the *simple-minded*. If you read through Proverbs, you'll see that this collection at first seems to have been put together for a young boy, probably a young teenager. While this adolescent was the initial reader, God obviously intended this book of wisdom to be useful for all of humanity in every generation.

The first application of *naive ones* would have to be young people who just haven't lived long enough to learn the important lessons of life. I have joked about how smart I was as a teenager and how dumb I became as an adult. We go through a matura-

> "How long, oh naïve ones, will you love being simple-minded?"
>
> Proverbs 1:22

tion process and come to understand how simple-minded we really were during those years where we once saw ourselves as so smart. Maturity brings with it an understanding of our own ignorance about life and other important matters.

Being naive or simple-minded is not just limited to our youth. The fact is that even the smartest among us lacks all of the important knowledge and understanding for successful living. Einstein once said that he knew less than one percent of everything that there is to know in life. Our ignorance and slow-mindedness is a challenge to the lessons of wisdom. Often times, understanding just slips right over our heads, even though Lady Wisdom is screaming for our attention. She asks how long we'll love being simple-minded. God is presenting us with the option of choosing wisdom over foolishness. How long will we be satisfied with being foolish?

The basic problem of a scoffer is pride, and we will find that pride is at the heart of every human being. It is the basic struggle of humanity and the one thing that causes people to reject God's offer of grace. Pride says to God, "I've got this. If I need your help, I'll let you know." The problem is that we desperately need God's help, and many times, we're too foolish to realize it.

The Crossroad

"The Road Not Taken" by Robert Frost, is one of my favorite poems. He writes as if he is walking through the woods and comes to a split in the road and has to decide which way to take. He ends it with these words:

Two roads diverged in a wood, and I—
I took the one less traveled by,
And that has made all the difference.

Think back to a time when you arrived at a crossroad and had to decide the best way to take. If you had GPS, the correct way may have been obvious, but let's assume that you were totally on your own. Because crossroads can be challenging, you have a fifty/fifty chance of making the right choice.

In the case of taking the wise path, we also have two options. One path leads to a life of blessing, and the other path of fools leads to destruction. Lady Wisdom pleads with us in Proverbs 1:23 to heed her call, *"Turn to my reproof. Behold, I will pour out my spirit on you; I will make my words known to you."* She sounds like an evangelist calling for repentance. The NIV translates the first word of the verse as *repent.* The Hebrew word literally means to *turn back* or *return.* It definitely carries with it the idea of repenting, which means to turn around and go in the other direction. It is as if Lady Wisdom recognizes that people are going in the wrong direction and is calling us to turn around and follow God.

We know that the scripture is speaking to those going in the wrong direction because of God's reproof. Isn't it interesting that God asks us to turn *to* His reproof? We can respond in one of two ways to God's discipline or correction. For those with a rebellious spirit, they will run from God with greater rebellion. For those with a repentant spirit, they will turn to God. When we turn to God, He responds by pouring out His Spirit on us and making His words known to us. An obvious part of fearing the Lord is responding in repentance to God's correction. When we repent, we open our hearts and minds up to the wisdom of God.

Proverbs 1:33 tells us that when we respond properly to God's reproof and choose the path of wisdom, we will *live securely.* Security is a major issue in our society. It was a significant factor in our last presidential election. According to the Institute for Policy Studies, we have spent a total of $6.7 million per hour for homeland security since 9/11. This statistic means that as I write this sentence, we have spent a total of $791,035,500,000 on homeland security since September 11, 2001. That number increases every second.[3] Americans spend over twenty billion dollars per year on home security systems. Security is obviously a big deal to us and to God. God says that when we choose the path of wisdom and respond properly to His reproof, we live securely. God's security is greater than anything our government offers.

> "Don't make a permanent decision for your temporary emotion."

While God wants us to choose the wise path at the crossroad, many people opt for the foolish path. Solomon describes the results of such foolishness with words like calamity, dread, distress, and anguish. He says, "Dread comes like a storm and calamity comes like a whirlwind" (Proverbs 1:27).

Think back to a time when you experienced a terrible storm. We've all seen the destruction of tornadoes and hurricanes. A tornado hit our neighborhood in 2011, and our house had some damage. A number of houses around us were destroyed, so we were very fortunate. Solomon said that the consequences of a life lived foolishly will be destructive indeed. Although he did not use the imagery of a storm, I think about the pieces of my roof littering my yard and connect them to the broken lives of people being impacted by foolish living.

God said that these foolish people *hated knowledge and did not choose the fear of the Lord* (Proverbs 1:29). They spurned God's reproof. We live in a time where people ignore consequences, but they ignore them at their own peril. Proverbs 1:31-32 speaks to the consequences of choosing the foolish path and ignoring the cry of Lady Wisdom:

> *So, they shall eat of the fruit of their own way*
> *And be satiated with their own devices.*
> *For the waywardness of the naive will kill them,*
> *And the complacency of fools will destroy them.*

FURTHER THOUGHT

- What challenges to wisdom's cry do you experience in your life?

- Do you find yourself living on the busy streets of stress and pressure? What makes your life so busy? Is your busy schedule keeping you from taking to heart God's call for wisdom? If so, what will you do about it?

- Do you find that pride gets in your way of following God? Pride led Adam and Eve to sin in the garden.

Where might it lead in your life? Write down a few
consequences of pride you might face in your life if
you continue on this path. Will you repent of your
pride today and humble yourself before God?

- Think back to a time when you stood at the crossroad
  of wisdom and foolishness. Which way did you take?
  What were the consequences?

- As you read this chapter, did God prompt you with a
  call to turn or repent? Did you? Will you?

CHAPTER FIVE
Folly's Plea

The woman of folly is boisterous,
*   she is naive and knows nothing.*
She sits at the doorway of her house,
*   on a seat by the high places of the city.*
Calling to those who pass by,
*   who are making their paths straight.*
"Whoever is naive, let him turn in here,"
*   and to him who lacks understanding she says,*
"Stolen water is sweet;
*   and bread eaten in secret is pleasant."*
But he does not know that the dead are there,
*   that her guests are in the depths of Sheol.*
—Proverbs 9:13-18

Oliver Wendell Holmes once said, "The sound of a kiss is not so loud as that of a cannon, but its echo lasts a great deal longer." We may find that the things in life that are of the greatest importance may be the most subtle and unobtrusive. Although in the last chapter, we saw that Lady Wisdom cried in the busy streets, many times, wisdom speaks very softly indeed. We have probably all experienced the gentle tug on our hearts to do the right thing or follow the right path.

Evil and folly are not so subtle. The things of evil typically scream for our attention and demand our focus. Satan has a way of making every temptation appealing; therefore, folly is crafty at occupying our gaze.

I mentioned previously that Solomon initially had a young, male reader in mind when he wrote his proverbs, so with a male reader in mind, he chose the imagery of women to be the voices of wisdom and folly. For those of us who are males, we may not want to admit it, but the women in our lives—our mothers, wives, and daughters—have a lot of power over us.

I'm not sure who first said it, but this phrase rings true: "If Mama ain't happy, ain't nobody happy." As a husband, I want to please my wife, and as a father of four daughters, I want to see smiles on the faces of my beautiful girls. I'm assuming that Solomon chose to make wisdom and folly feminine because of the affect females can have on males. Lady Wisdom may have shouted in the busy streets, but in this chapter, we'll see where her counterpart, Lady Folly, will work to get the attention of those who pass by her.

We are moving over several chapters in Proverbs to the ninth because I want us to see the tug-of-war being played where Team Wisdom pulls on one side and Team Folly pulls on the other. We are the first person on Team Wisdom who will be pulled into the pit by our opponent—only this pit consists of more than just mud. These two options, wisdom and folly, define for us our choice at the crossroads of life, and they summarize much of the message of Proverbs.

Notice how Lady Folly is introduced in Proverbs 9:13, *"The woman of folly is boisterous, she is naive and knows nothing."* Foolishness is depicted as a woman who is ignorant, yet she works her wiles to pull others down into the pit with her. Solomon has depicted Lady Folly as a woman devoid of high standards and godly morality. He presents folly and sin as a woman sitting at her door with reckless immodesty and working hard to draw people into her net of sin and shame.

While the New American Standard Bible translated the Hebrew word *hahmah* with the term *boisterous*, other translations have opted for words such as *loud, clamorous, unruly,* and *brash*. Even though this fictional woman lacked intelligence, she was loud and seemingly a bit out of control. After reading this passage, I imagined someone in a drunken stupor acting out his or her unrestrained desire. This passage also brought back a memory of a woman I once saw on Bourbon Street in New Orleans. We went there to share the gospel in street evangelism, and I felt like I was standing at the door of hell. This woman was scantily dressed doing her best to lure people through the door into what I was sure was a place of debauchery. Folly has no regard for other people

> **"A prudent man conceals knowledge, but the heart of fools proclaim folly."**
>
> Proverbs 12:23

or principles, but rather, it always demands an audience. How many times has a foolish thought demanded attention in your mind?

The fact that folly lacks mental substance should not be a surprise to us. Solomon presented the idea that Lady Folly didn't know anything. If this were a real woman, would it be accurate to say that she knew nothing? Of course not. Everyone knows *something*. When these words were penned, the writer couldn't have meant that this imaginary woman knew absolutely nothing. Her naivete had to point to her lack of understanding or concern about consequences. She lived totally in the moment with no care about what might happen in response to her demands.

Isn't this behavior reminiscent of sin? Temptation never focuses on future consequences but rather on initial fulfillment. Commercials for alcohol never show the wino in the streets or the physically abused family of an alcoholic. Sin never wants us to look ahead. Lady Folly's focus was the moment and not the future. She was clueless about the outcome of sin.

Folly's Plan of Attack

Solomon said that Lady Folly sat *at the doorway of her house*. Isn't that an interesting contrast? Lady Wisdom shouted in the streets and lifted her voice in the square, but Lady Folly never left home. For Folly's work to be done, we must walk her way. I thought of the words of James 1:14-15: "But each one is tempted when he is carried away and enticed by his own lust. Then when lust has conceived, it gives birth to sin; and when sin is accomplished, it brings forth death."

Did you catch that truth? We can't blame other people for our spiritual and moral failures. We can't even blame Satan. This thought brings to my mind the words of comedian Flip Wilson, "The Devil made me do it." Here's a biblical memo: *No one makes us sin but ourselves*. We can't blame the Devil. We can't blame our parents, our enemies, or our friends. It's kind of like what I once heard, "If I could kick the person most responsible for all of my troubles, I wouldn't be able to sit down for a week." We are at fault. Lady Folly doesn't have to go out screaming into the city streets in order to get our attention because we walk down her street in the shadow of her house. We might even walk up on her front porch and sit down beside her in a rocking chair.

Why don't we take a different street? Possibly because we have a false sense of security. We think that we would never get sucked in by Folly's ploys, but the truth is believers fall every day. We either see ourselves as spiritually superior to Lady Folly and therefore having super willpower, or we just don't think about the power of sin at all.

It's possible that we wander through life without spiritual awareness and don't realize the power of evil around us. We may even have developed a sense of spiritual callousness that has created an apathetic attitude toward sin and holiness. Regardless of the reasons for our failures, God has given us a strong warning and the opportunity to choose the right path.

This passage says not only that Lady Folly will sit at the doorway of her house, but also, she will sit *on a seat by the high places of the city*. In this allegory, Solomon is stating that Lady Folly's house is constructed in a prominent place in the city. We have probably all learned that it is easy to find foolishness and sin in life. While we may have to work to

> "In the way of righteousness is life, and in its pathway, there is no death."
>
> Proverbs 12;28

gain knowledge and study to ascertain wisdom, folly and sin are quite simple to find. As water always naturally flows downhill, humanity easily runs into foolishness. You can probably imagine a father trying to convince his son to avoid the simple path that leads to folly and choose the more challenging way of wisdom.

In your case, you may be the father or the mother and not the son. The message is still just as important. The path to sin and folly is simple to follow, regardless of our age. The only problem with that path is that it is crowded because most people ignore the invitation of Lady Wisdom. God's challenge to us is to choose the path to wisdom, even if it means that we walk that path alone. In time, we will find other sojourners who have chosen the wise path of obedience and submission to God's ways.

Notice that Proverbs 9:15 says that folly calls to those *who are making their paths straight*. Isn't that interesting? It doesn't say that folly is screaming for the attention of those who are already ruining their lives. Instead, Lady Folly is after fresh "blood." She wants those who are living right and choosing the right path. Her goal is to sidetrack someone who otherwise is seeking to follow the Lord. How does she go about this? Her strategy is simple: deception.

Lady Folly promises that sin is sweet, and secret sin is pleasant. It is the invitation to a double life where sin is pursued in the recesses of our minds or the dark places of our solitude. It is the promise of enjoyment and accomplishment. Sin always promises fulfillment. It always offers momentary sweetness where, in fact, there is lasting bitterness. The passerby has no idea that Lady Folly is actually leading him to the grave. When the scripture pointed out that *the dead are there*, it underscores the destructive nature of sin and folly. The word *Sheol* means the place where the dead go. It can point to the underworld, or more specifically the grave. The underlying message is that folly always leads to destruction.

Proverbs presents guidance for a number of subjects, but the overall message is clear. Life offers us two paths: the path of wisdom and the path of folly. Be careful. Choose wisely. The path of wisdom leads to great blessing, but the path of folly leads to great sorrow.

- When was the last time you heard the boisterous voice of Lady Folly? How did you respond?

- Think of a time that you gave in to temptation's pull. Did you find initial fulfillment but eventual despair? Think of how fulfilling it would have been to please the Lord instead of cave to sin's enticement.

- Have you ever blamed someone else for your sin? How do you respond to the message of James 1:14-15 that says you are responsible for your sin? It is a lot easier to blame other people or circumstances, but the bottom line is that we are responsible for our failures. How does this truth affect what you do with temptation?

- While a lot of roads lead past the home of Lady Folly, some roads bypass her house altogether. What would you have to do daily to choose different roads than those which lead in the shadow of her house? Will you take a different path?

CHAPTER SIX
Wisdom's Reward

A couple of years ago, I reviewed my retirement account to determine whether or not I should make some changes. The obvious change needed was more money in the account. We probably all wish we had started sooner and invested more money. I jokingly told someone that I could retire at seventy-years-old, but I'd have to die at seventy-three. Knowing that I couldn't go back to the past, I focused on the future. I need my account to bring me the best return possible, so I went about studying other potential funds that would bring greater reward.

God presents wisdom's reward throughout the book of Proverbs, but chapter three addresses the topic in some detail. Look at Proverbs 3:13-18:

> *How blessed is the man who finds wisdom*
> *   And the man who gains understanding.*
> *For her profit is better than the profit of silver*
> *   And her gain better than fine gold.*
> *She is more precious than jewels;*
> *   And nothing you desire compares with her.*
> *Long life is in her right hand;*
> *   In her left hand are riches and honor.*
> *Her ways are pleasant ways*

And all her paths are peace.
She is a tree of life to those who take hold of her,
And happy are all who hold her fast.

Wisdom's Happiness

Verse thirteen reminds me of Psalm 1:1 "How blessed is the man who does not walk in the counsel of the wicked," or Jesus' words in the Sermon on the Mount, "Blessed are the poor in spirit, for theirs is the Kingdom of heaven." The word blessed is a common word in Christian circles. We often hear, "God bless you," or "I am so blessed." I once heard a dear saint say, "I'm too blessed to be distressed." That's not a bad motto. However, what do we really mean when we use the word blessed?

> "Blessed" implies an inner satisfaction and sufficiency that did not depend on outward circumstances for happiness.

Even though Jesus' words were recorded in Greek, and Proverbs was written in Hebrew, the word we see translated as blessed means basically the same thing regardless of the two languages. In both cases, it carries the idea of being happy or joyful; therefore, Solomon began discussing the reward of wisdom by saying, "How happy or joyful is the man who finds wisdom." We will look at some proverbs dealing with happiness in another chapter, but God is pointing out to us in this passage that one of the underlying rewards of wisdom is abiding joy and blissful happiness.

Notice the parallelism used in verse thirteen. This passage speaks of the man who finds wisdom and the man who gains understanding. Although wisdom and understanding carry a slightly different meaning, it seems that the writer is thinking somewhat synonymously. Words are important, and I believe strongly that God inspired the words of Scripture and not just the thoughts. In the case of Hebrew poetry, we may see the writer not so focused on the detailed meaning of a word as with the connection of that term to a previous thought. In this case, understanding is used to expand the meaning of wisdom. In chapter two, I wrote of couplets that express completion. Proverbs 3:13 is an example of this type of couplet. Gaining wisdom means that our understanding of a situation is expanded, and we see the full ramifications of a circumstance. So, the person who has this wisdom and understanding will experience great happiness.

Measuring Wisdom's Worth

Why does the person who finds wisdom and understanding experience great joy? It is because wisdom's profit is immense—immeasurable even. Notice how Solomon moves to the terminology or economics of an investor. These are terms reminiscent of the board room of a business or of a stock broker's office on Wall Street. God speaks of profit and gain. He led Solomon to tell us that the profit of wisdom is *better than silver*. He said *the gain is better than fine gold*.

We all understand the value of silver and gold and its
worth to the overall economics of society. Depending

> "An excellent wife,
> who can find? For
> her worth is far
> above jewels."
> Proverbs 31:10

upon your perspective, you may
first think of silver and gold for
their beauty and not their worth.
Silver and gold are used in jewelry in part because they are
beautiful. Think for a moment
about the beauty of a life well
lived. If you have children, imagine them applying wisdom
to their lives and how their choices will ultimately sparkle
amidst the dullness of our society.

Consider the beauty of the lives of your grown children who have been brought up to build their lives upon
the truths of God's Word. They will live in a world where
broken families and busted up lives are normal, but their
wholeness will shine as a witness to an all-wise God. They
will look like the beautiful bloom of a desert flower in the
middle of a barren world. Before you move on to think
about the economic symbolism of silver and gold, ponder
the beauty of a life where understanding is normal, and
wisdom is applied to all circumstances and relation-ships.

Not only are silver and gold beautiful, but also valuable—valuable to the owner and to the people impacted
by the owner. We have probably all seen the advertise-
ments on television touting the benefits of investing in
gold and silver. The values of these two precious metals
continue to go up, but they cannot compare to the value
of wisdom. Referring to wisdom, verse fifteen says, "No-

thing you desire compares with her." That is quite a statement. *Nothing!* Think for a moment of all the things you desire. God tells us that nothing that runs through our mind, whether those things are desperate needs or lavish wants, can even begin to compare to the awesome and unimaginable worth of wisdom.

How can God say that nothing compares with her? Obviously, He can say it because He is God, but think for a moment about what would lead Him to make such a statement. Verses 16-18 provide part of the answer. God tells us that wisdom offers *long life* in one hand and *riches and honor* in the other. Wisdom also directs us down *pleasant ways*, and God says that *all her paths are peace*. Wow! Those are some powerful statements. I do not believe that God is saying that if you pursue Him, you are going to be rich. Riches and honor are often times found in things other than financial gain. I look at my beautiful family, the privilege I have to serve a wonderful church, the joy of influencing people through various avenues of ministry, the bounty of friends, and the amazing experiences I enjoy on a regular basis, and I would say that I am a wealthy man indeed.

Let's pause on the promise of peace that wisdom offers. Anytime I hear someone use the word *all*, the cynic in me pops up his head and doubts the authenticity of whatever follows that little three-letter word. In this case, the person saying it is God. Does God really mean *all*, or is this phrase one of those general proverbial statements that offers principles of truth? As you turn through the pages of Scripture, you see quickly that peace is not only the path on which we walk, but also it is the house in which we live. In Philippians 4:7, Paul called it a *peace which surpasses all comprehension,* while in Psalm 29:11, God says, "The Lord will bless His people with peace."

Is this type of peace really possible for you? Remember that fear of the Lord is the beginning of knowledge (Pr. 1:7) and wisdom (Pr. 9:10). To fear the Lord is to respect Him, revere Him, and to worship Him. It is a statement of devotion, adoration, and surrender. To fear the Lord is to have Him ever on your mind and in your heart.

> "Her ways are pleasant ways, and all her paths are peace."
> Proverbs 3:17

Isaiah 26:3 states, "You keep him in perfect peace whose mind is stayed on You, because he trusts in You" (ESV). Wisdom comes from fearing the Lord, which results in God being ever on our minds, and it leads to perfect peace, all peace at all times.

Verse eighteen tells us that wisdom is a tree of life, but it only brings life to those who *take hold of her.* This statement points to initiative and desire. Do you desire wisdom? Are you willing to take steps in order to take hold of her? When you hold to wisdom for dear life, you will find great happiness and contentment, but when you let go of wisdom and pursue folly, the end result is chaos and sorrow.

FURTHER THOUGHT

- Spend a moment reflecting on your life. While I know that you are blessed, would you say that you are blessed according to the definition mentioned at the beginning of this chapter? What are the evidences that your life is filled with happiness and joy? Would other people describe you as happy or joyful?

- Would you say that you are a person who has found wisdom and understanding? If not, what are you doing to pursue it?

- Have you ever tried to calculate wisdom's worth? Make a list of why wisdom is more valuable than gold and silver.

- Create another list of things that you desire. God says that nothing you desire compares to wisdom. Think through your list and try to determine how wisdom and understanding are greater than anything you could want.

- Would you say that your life is described as peaceful? How does it make you feel to think that your ways could be pleasant and all of your paths could be peace? What steps would you need to take to pursue wisdom and therefore experience peace?

- God told us that we will need to take hold of wisdom. This statement implies some effort and determination are needed to accomplish this task. What about you?

Are you determined to take hold of wisdom and hold on for dear life?

CHAPTER SEVEN
A Friend Indeed

"Sometimes you want to go where everybody knows your name." The chorus to the popular sitcom of the 80's, Cheers, reminds of the reality that God made us for friendship. We currently have over 327 million people living in the United States, which means if Americans stood shoulder-to-shoulder, we could circle the globe almost four times. That's a lot of people, yet according to one study, 40% - 45% of Americans are lonely.[4]

Should we be surprised that loneliness is growing in our modern-day where we communicate with 140 characters, call someone our "friend" whom we've met only on social media, and "unfriend" someone who disagrees with our opinion about something, such as school violence or because...well, you don't know why? Michael Bader calls loneliness in America a "deadly epidemic."[5] Do you find yourself lonelier today than you were ten years ago?

Our technology-driven society is moving us toward isolation, but God has made us for community. Christian author and psychologist Larry Crabb stated, "As our lungs require air, so our souls require what only community provides. We were designed by our Trinitarian God (who is Himself a group of three persons in profound relationship with each other) to live in relationship. Without it, we die. It's that simple."[6]

I'm concerned that while authors such as Crabb or preachers such as myself say that we need community or talk about friendship, we do not really understand what the words mean anymore. I can tell you how many friends I have on Facebook, but are they really my friends?

Foundation Blocks for Friendship

God has given us guidance about friendship in Proverbs and helps us to understand what it means to be a friend. Although Proverbs covers a number of topics, we're going to see that relationships are one of the top issues God addresses. You'll see guidance as it relates to relationships in our homes, our workplaces, and our communities. Look at a general statement about relation-ships Proverbs 3:3-4 that gives us some foundational thoughts for friendship:

> *Do not let kindness and truth leave you;*
> *Bind them around your neck,*
> *Write them on the tablet of your heart.*
> *So you will find favor and good repute in the sight of God*
> *and man.*

The word translated as *kindness* is one of my favorite Hebrew words: *hesed*. The NIV translates the word as *love*, while the KJV translators opted for *mercy*. Although these words are good translations, the rich meaning behind the word opens our understanding of this critical quality needed in our relationships. This word describes God's relationship with Israel, and by extension, His relationship with His church. *Hesed* is not just describing mercy or kindness, but it was also a "loyalty to His covenant obligations."[7] The word communicates a steadfastness and consistency that is tied to God's divine nature. You may consider the word *hesed* as

> If we mistake God's silence for indifference, we are the most miserable of people. If we give up when we no longer understand, we reject His caring, steadfast love and cut ourselves off from our only real hope.
>
> Sheila Walsh

the Old Testament equivalent to *God is love*. The English Standard Version translates Lamentations 3:22 as "The steadfast love of the Lord never ceases; His mercies never come to an end." God's *hesed* is a steadfast love for us that cannot be quenched or minimized. God can never love you more, and God can never love you less. His love is profound, loyal, immeasurable, and incomprehensible. Maybe that's one reason that the Apostle Paul said, "Love never fails" (1 Corinthians 13:8).

In Proverbs 3:3, God tells us not to let kindness, or *hesed*, leave us. This type of love is the foundation of friendship and every other relationship known to humanity. The New Testament equivalent would be the Greek word *agape*, a love that is selfless and lasting, sacrificial and lavish. Proverbs 17:17 states, "A friend loves at all times, and a brother is born for adversity." As we look at other aspects of friendship from Proverbs, let's remember that it must be built upon a kindness that runs deep through the heart of loyalty and steadfastness.

Even as loyal love is a building block to abiding friendships, truth is just as important. Truth and kindness are like two sides of the same coin, identical twins, or a braided cord. They simply go together. Truth is an essential concept in Bible doctrine and is at the heart of our understanding of faith. You will find that some translators preferred the word *faithfulness* (ESV & NIV for example) because the root word carries with it the idea of certainty. It could be used to the describe the strong arms of a man supporting his ailing friend. When God inspired Solomon to combine the concepts of kindness and truth, He wanted us to realize the importance of a love that is always dependable.

We think of dependable as always being present or able to accomplish a task. The word would also mean faithful to be honest or to speak truth This Hebrew

> "A friend loves at all times, and a brother is born for adversity."
>
> Proverbs 17:17

word is tied to faith because it is built upon assurance of something or someone being dependable or true. The bottom line is that real friends will not let you down, and real friends will always be honest. Can you see how these two qualities are essential for meaningful friendship?

Do you see the command in this passage? Do not let these two qualities leave you! They are a key component to real Christian community. Bind them around your neck as a reminder (sort of like tying a string around your finger) and write them on your heart. Writing them on your heart carries the idea of engraving these concepts in stone so they will always be true of your relationships. Kindness and truth should be permanent features of your life and of your relationships. These qualities lead to favor and a good reputation with God and people.

Choose Your Friends Carefully

Life is all about choices. Motivational speaker Tony Robbins stated, "Your life changes the moment you make a new, congruent, and committed decision." One of the most important decisions you will make is your choice of friends. Our friends affect us in powerful ways. Consider the wisdom of Proverbs 13:20, "He who walks with wise men will be wise, but the companion of fools will suffer harm." Maybe George Washington had this proverb in mind when he said, "It is better to be alone than in bad company." Goethe once said, "Tell me with whom you associate, and I will tell you who you are."

God warned us in Proverbs 13:20 to choose our friends well. I have determined that there are three types of people in life. There are those who replenish you, and there are those who drain you. The third type are those who are eager to learn from you and in whom you are pouring yourself, so hopefully, you too are a replenisher.

This proverb presents process and consequence. In this case, the process involves making a choice with whom you will spend time. Who will be your close friends or your mentors? The first illustration highlights the person who chooses to *walk* with wise people. When you spend a lot of time with wise people, you will learn from them and gain greater understanding.

The second option is being a companion of fools. When a person chooses to spend a lot of time with foolish people, harm is surely the outcome. Remember, "The fear of the Lord is the beginning of wisdom" (Proverbs 9:10).

> "He who walks with wise men will be wise, but the companion of fools will suffer harm."
>
> Proverbs 13:20

If a person chooses to spend time with foolish people, his companions are those who do not fear the Lord. People who do not fear the Lord not only do foolish things but also do immoral things. Is it any wonder that God says that those who are companions with fools will suffer harm? While there is an eternal consequence for sin, there is also an earthly consequence.

This couplet offers parallelism on several levels. The first is the synonymous use of *walk* with *companion*. The second example of parallelism is a contrast between wise men and fools. The third contrast relates to the consequence: wisdom versus harm.

The consequence of being a companion of the wise is reiterated in Proverbs 27:17: "Iron sharpens iron, so one man sharpens another." In this case, a wise man is compared to iron. The insinuation is that two people learning from each other and growing together are like two pieces of iron rubbing together. The two pieces end up becoming sharper. Whenever we spend time with people who replenish us, and we replenish them, we will grow sharper and more useful for the Kingdom of God. If you want to be a better leader, spend time with strong leaders. If you want to be a stronger person of prayer, then spend time with strong prayer warriors and go before the throne of God with your friend in prayer.

Think about the application of this principle to parenting. I do not intend to offend any young people who may be reading this book, but the fact is that a young person does not have as much wisdom or knowledge as people in their thirties, forties, fifties, or higher. This truth has nothing to with intelligence, but it has everything to do with life experience. Time well spent and contemplated is one of life's greatest teachers.

One of the jobs of parenting is to keep our children from being the companion of fools. If you are a parent, you can choose to have a hands-off type of approach to the friends your children choose but know that you be assisting your children as they stroll down the path toward harm and destruction. If we want our children to live a blessed life and gain wisdom for daily living, we must help them develop friendships that will be like iron sharpening iron. I'll deal more with parenting in another chapter, but

we must be involved in our children's lives in order to
influence them in their choice of friends.

Think about the meaning of Proverbs 27:17 in your
own life. We all need close friends in our lives who will
help us to be better people.
Think about the relation-
ship between David and
Jonathan. They were best
friends—like iron sharpening iron. In 1 Samuel 23, we
read the story where David
was fleeing from King Saul.

> "As our lungs require air, so our souls require what only community provides."
>
> Larry Crabb

Jonathan, King Saul's son and the next in line to be king,
was David's close friend and ally. Verse sixteen states,
"And Jonathan, Saul's son, arose and went to David at
Horesh and encouraged him in God." We need friends
like that in our lives, and we need to be friends like that to
someone else.

In 1981, nine physically handicapped people con-
quered Mount Rainier. One of them had an artificial leg.
Another was an epileptic. Two were deaf, and five were
blind. They hiked over glaciers and survived falling ice.
Once they topped the 14,410-foot mountain, they joined
hands, walked across the summit, and signed the logbook
on the top of one of the tallest mountains in the United
States. When a reporter asked them how they managed to
perform such an amazing feat, one of the blind members
of the party said, "We had a lot of help from each other
on the trip."[8]

We all have mountains we want to climb, and climbing those mountains requires personal growth. Hopefully, we'll be smarter next year than we are this year. We should grow spiritually, intellectually, emotionally, and relationally. Remember that God made us for community, and one reason we need community is so that we will become the strong, mature people that God intends us to be. If you want to grow in positive ways in your life, then I suggest you make plans now as to how you will spend time with wise people. How will you find another person who is like iron to you so that by this time next year you will be a sharper person?

FURTHER THOUGHT

- Do you have many close friends in your life? If not, why not?

- Think about the building blocks of kindness and truth. How have you seen those two crucial elements in your relationships with other people?

- If you do not have close friends, think about someone you know who has a close friend. Do they demonstrate loyalty?

- As it relates to friendship, what does it mean for you to bind truth around your neck and write it on your heart?

- Have you experienced the pain of suffering harm because you chose to make fools your companions? Have you ever experienced the benefit of becoming friends with a wise person?

- What will you do in the future to make sure that your path does not lead you to harm?

- What are some things you can do to find a friend who is like iron in your life? Would you be willing to be a part of a small group of Christian friends who are determined to help one another grow?

CHAPTER EIGHT
Adversity: Friend or Foe?

You have probably heard the quote that says, "Nothing in this world is certain but death and taxes." That quote is not exactly true. There is at least a third certainty: adversity. We can be as sure of struggle and adversity as we are of rain in the spring. The question is not "Will I have adversity?" but rather "What will I do when adversity comes?" We can flee adversity, but when we turn to look behind us, we will find adversity has commenced the chase and will soon overcome us. In the third act of William Shakespeare's Henry VI, the king expressed his conclusion with what to do with adversity: "Let me embrace thee, sour adversity, for wise men say it is the wisest course."

Adversity's Certainty

Proverbs 24:10 states, "If you are slack in the day of distress, your strength is limited." Notice that this proverb does not say, "If you have a day of distress," but rather it underscores the reality that distress is commonplace in our lives. Regardless of how long we have lived on planet Earth, we have all experienced times of *distress, adversity* (KJV) or *trouble* (NIV). The root of this word in Hebrew refers to being in a narrow or constricted place. When was the last time you were squeezed by difficult times in your life? Distress can be something as simple as misplacing our shoes or something as challenging as a bad report from the doctor.

The Bible has much to say about adversity. James 1:2 tells us to consider it joy *when* we have times of trials. Paul offers a partial resume of his adversity in 2 Corinthians 11:24-25, when he writes, "Five times I received from the Jews thirty-nine lashes. Three times I was beaten with rods, once I was stoned, three times I was shipwrecked, a night and a day I have spent in the deep." Not only is that a testimony of adversity but also of perseverance. A little earlier in his second letter to the Corinthians, he reminded his readers to expect adversity:

But we have this treasure in earthen vessels, so that the surpassing greatness of the power will be of God and not from ourselves; we are afflicted in every way, but not crushed; perplexed, but not despairing; persecuted, but not forsaken; struck down, but not destroyed; always carrying about in the body the dying of Jesus, so that the life of Jesus also may be manifested in our body.

—2 Corinthians 4:7-10

What can we glean about adversity and how to deal with it from the book of Proverbs? The proverb mentioned above not only reminds us that *distress* is normal, it also challenges us not to be *slack* when facing adversity. Have you ever felt like giving up? Have you felt like your problems were so stacked against you that you were going to drown? Instead of fighting to keep your head above water, you just wanted to let go and sink. Can you relate to being *slack in the day of distress*?

You may think of a variety of reasons for being *slack* or wanting to give up while facing trouble, but the bottom line reason is that *your strength is limited*. Does that statement seem to be a little obvious? Even the strongest people have their limitations. Before we write this proverb off as too obvious, take a moment to let the truth steep in your kettle of knowledge. The first word of the proverb is telling: *if*. This little two letter word is presenting possibilities and options. To say, "If you are slack" means that not being slack is an option.

If we are *not* slack or faint while facing adversity, it means that we are strong. What is the variable of this proverb? The *day of distress* is not an option. Those days are coming. You may even be facing one right now. The variable is strength. If you faint when adversity comes, as the ESV translates, it is because you are not strong. What kind of strength is required for adversity? It is probably not referencing physical strength. As a matter of fact, I have seen some physically strong people wilt in the face of trouble. This passage points to something greater than physical strength, something that must underscore emotional and spiritual fortitude.

> "Kites fly highest against the wind - not with it."
>
> Winston Churchill

My wife is one of the strongest people I know, but I guarantee you that I can bench press at least triple what she can, probably quadruple. She just recently went through two surgeries that would make strong men weep, and she has come through with flying colors. I wish I had counted the number of times someone in the hospital made reference to her being so small. The thought has occurred to me that it may not be that she is so small, but rather that everyone else is so big. Sandra has been very diet and health conscious for quite some time and has given a lot of thought to the kinds of foods that feed diseases such as cancer. When she asked her doctor if there was any type of food she should add to her diet, he said, "Yes. Biscuits."

The strength this proverb is talking about has nothing to do with muscle mass or body size. It has everything to do with the size of your spiritual vitality and emotional stability. Because we make daily decisions about spiritual disciplines, spiritual fitness is optional, and many people struggle with emotional stability. Sadly, most Christians are spirit-

> "Sow a thought, reap an action; sow an action, reap a habit; sow a habit, reap a character; sow a character, reap a destiny."
>
> Ralph Waldo Emmerson

ually flabby. Most of us do not spend time strengthening our spiritual muscles through Bible reading, prayer, Christian fellowship, worship, and active service.

Are you *slack in the day of distress*? If so, it is because you are spiritually weak. I know that is a tough pill to swallow. It would feel better if God would have given us some other options, but on the front end of adversity, God would rather us feel strong than better. So, what will you do about the state of your spiritual fitness?

Adversity's Purpose

I have been a Christian for a long time, and I have learned that God is never haphazard nor surprised. Has it ever occurred to you that nothing ever occurs to God? He is totally aware of why something happened yesterday and about what will happen tomorrow. In God's economy, there are no benign experiences; instead, every experience is an opportunity for the glory of God to spread through our lives and spill over into our world. Life is filled with one divine appointment after another with hardship and challenges where God is orchestrating opportunities for us to grow to be more like His Son.

In Romans 8:29, we sometimes get hung up on the words *foreknew* and *predestined* and miss the whole point of the verse: "For those whom He foreknew, He also predestined to become conformed to the image of His Son." Because God knows all things, doesn't it make a lot of sense that God knows ahead of time who will become a Christian? The focus of this verse is on the fact that God's plan is for Christians to become conformed to, or take on the qualities of, Jesus. God's first goal for your life is for you to become a believer, and His second goal is for you to become like His Son.

Proverbs 17:3 underscores the purpose of adversity, "The refining pot is for silver and the furnace for gold, but the Lord tests hearts." This proverb offers both a contrast and a comparison. The contrast is between silver and gold and the heart, and the comparison is testing and refining. Let's consider the imagery of this couplet.

Both silver and gold can be found in its native, pure form, but it is usually mined in pieces of ore or other sulfides. In order to separate the gold or silver from the other impurities, the ore will need to be refined through either *the refining pot* or *furnace*. Heat is applied to remove the impurities. God compares our times of suffering to the heat of the refining process.

> "But He knows the way I take; when He has tried me, I shall come forth as gold."
>
> Job 23:10

Buried deep down within our lives is a quality that is more valuable and beautiful than gold and silver. The impurities of sin and unhealthy habits, however, hide the beautiful brilliance of this precious, spiritual metal. The Lord takes us through a refining process to remove the impurities that keep us from shining the glorious radiance of God in our lives. God likens this process to the *refining pot* and the *furnace*. While in our modern day there may be other steps and chemicals used in this process, we know that in biblical times the focus was upon heat.

This type of heat can show up in various ways in our lives. It may be the heat of hardship and loss, or it could be the heat of relational struggle or even failure. Sometimes the heat is of our own making, while at other times, other people create the friction in our lives. Isaiah 48:10 addressed God's refining process, "Behold, I have refined you, but not as silver; I have tested you in the furnace of affliction." God is clear in this passage that our struggles and other afflictions have great spiritual value. God uses them like a refiner's fire.

Maybe Shakespeare's King Henry VI was correct by saying he wanted to embrace adversity, even though it is sour. Adversity can shape us like nothing else can in life. We can probably all compare times of great struggle in our lives as well as times of great peace. In which time did you grow the most? Rick Warren said, "God is more interested in your character than your comfort. God is more interested in making your life holy than He is in making your life happy."[9] God wants to change your life, but He has given you the freedom to choose whether or not to respond to His promptings. Will you give God permission to shape your character by making you more uncomfortable?

Adversity's Community

Adversity moves us toward isolation. Why is it that the very thing we need during times of distress is the one thing from which we may run? I have often times compared life of humanity in the world to the lives of animals on the

African plain. Lions find the one, lone gazelle that has wandered from the rest of the herd to attack. Satan is the same way. He works in our hearts to separate us from community, and then we become prey for his wicked schemes. While facing adversity, we must run toward community.

Proverbs 17:17 speaks to the value of real community, "A friend loves at all times, and a brother is born for adversity." This proverb contains a powerful truth from two perspectives. The first view comes from the perspective of a friend seeing his brother facing adversity. This friend *loves at all times.* The world shows us how to love when our friends are healthy and able to love us back, but a true friend's love is constant.

I have noticed a phenomenon that must break the heart of God. Christians shoot their wounded. No, we do not physically kill those who have been wounded, but

> "Bear one another's burdens, and thereby fulfill the law of Christ."
>
> Galatians 6:2

what we often times do may be worse. Instead of helping a Christian brother who has fallen because of sin or struggle, we sometimes turn our backs on them. Many times, we do worse than that when we talk about them in critical ways to other people. There is a reason why Scripture speaks strongly against gossip and slander. Gossip and slander run just as rampant through the church as it does the world. This behavior should not be!

Please do not hear me say that we should never confront Christians in their sin and call them to repentance. Bible verses like Galatians 6:1 and Luke 17:3 challenge us to be willing to go to someone who has sinned, confront them, and help them to return to Christ. James 5:19-20 reminds us that this act of love is incredibly important:

My brethren, if any among you strays from the truth and one turns him back, let him know that he who turns a sinner from the error of his way will save his soul from death and will cover a multitude of sins.

Proverbs 17:17 challenges us to be a true friend. When someone falls into the mud of failure and despair, we get into the mud and pull them out. I am convinced that we sometimes fall into sin that is very difficult to overcome by ourselves. When we do, we need our Christian friends in order to live a victorious life.

This passage also speaks to the person in adversity. It reminds us that our Christian brothers exist to help us during our times of trouble. This passage is a constant reminder that we should reach out to our friends for help. They were born for this type of ministry. We must not face adversity alone. We have great strength when we stand together in community.

FURTHER THOUGHT

- Can you relate to the issue of distress or trouble in your life? Think back to the last time you faced distress. What was the issue?

- Have you ever faced distress and found your strength waning? What did you do?

- What are some things you can do to build your spiritual muscles? Take some time to write out a list of steps you will take in the next month to help yourself to become spiritually stronger.

- How has God used adversity in your life to grow you to be more like Jesus? Read James 1:2-4 and Romans 5:3-5. Share with someone this week how God has used difficult times to shape your life in positive ways.

- Have you noticed that gossip seems to be normal in the lives of people, regardless of whether or not they are Christians? Do you have a problem with gossip or slander? If so, would you be willing to repent of it now and commit yourself to being an encourager instead of a slanderer?

- What can you do to be a real friend to someone in need right now?

CHAPTER NINE
Do Diligence

"You can do anything you want to do if you want to do it badly enough." I heard my mother say those words a thousand times. It was her challenge to me to dream, to persevere, and to work hard. Unfortunately, in the United States today, hard work has become a lost commodity for many. Some years ago, *The Daily Beast* ran an article about the laziest countries in the world as if the top twenty-four developed countries in the world were in a contest called The Couch Potato Olympics. Guess who won first place? You guessed it. The United States brought home the gold. The writer said, "Just like in the real Olympics, where America is jockeying to hold on to the medal lead, America always goes big or doesn't go at all."[10] I smiled when I read the opening paragraphs of the article, but maybe I should have wept.

Has laziness really become the norm for our citizens? To be fair, a lot of people work really hard. You may be the hardest worker in the country, but many people today opt for the easy way out. One evidence of the lack of initiative to go the extra mile is the decrease in ambition among new business owners. Business formation statistics from the U. S. Census Bureau show that fewer people are starting businesses today than ten years ago.[11]

Physical health, or the lack of it, is another area where laziness becomes obvious. According to the National Health and Nutrition Examination Survey, more than two out of three adults in the United States were considered to be overweight or obese.[12] It doesn't take official statistics to know that we have a problem. Just look around. We might could even look in the mirror. My friend Steve Reynolds, author of *Bod 4 God*, once said, "What you eat in private you wear in public." If you happen to live in a country other than the United States, you will find that the citizens there have a natural tendency toward laziness and poor health, too.

What is the problem? While the issues are multifaceted, it is ultimately a spiritual problem. We are told in the 1 Corinthians 6:19-20 that our bodies are the temple of God. We are also challenged throughout the Scripture to be hard workers for God's glory. In Proverbs, God used an illustration from nature to call us to diligence.

Go to the ant, O sluggard,
   Observe her ways and be wise
Which, having no chief, officer or ruler,
   Prepares her food in the summer and gathers her provision in
   the harvest.
How long will you lie down, O sluggard?
   When will you arise from your sleep?
A little sleep, a little slumber,
   a little folding of the hands to rest
Your poverty will come in like a vagabond

and your need like an armed man.
                    —Proverbs 6:6-11

Big Lessons from Little Creatures

"Go to the ant." When is the last time you gave any thought to an ant? The little insect has probably not entered your mind since you accidentally stepped in an ant bed or found a family of them working on your picnic lunch before you had a chance to eat it yourself. If you study ants, you will find that they are fascinating little insects. It is difficult simply to talk about an ant because there are over 12,000 different species of ants all over the world. These insects are community oriented, which means they live in colonies with sometimes millions of other ants.

Did you know that an ant can pick up twenty times its body weight? That would be like a twelve-year-old picking up a small car. When God inspired Solomon to say, "Go to the ant" or as the New Living Translation says, "Take a lesson from the ants," he was saying a lot. Although we can learn many interesting things about this creature, the focus of Solomon's thoughts was on the ant's diligence. He called us to *observe her ways and be wise*. Solomon is not so interested in the ant's characteristics or the amazing feats this little insect can accomplish. He is most concerned

> *"The hand of the diligent will rule, but the slack hand will be put to forced labor."*
>
> Proverbs 12:24

with the *ways* of an ant. Specifically, he is laser beam focused on the diligence of the ant.

The point of Solomon's words is not to analyze the life of an ant as if we are entomologists, but rather to look at this creature from a normal human being's perspective. Consider the fact that an ant does not appear to have a task master commanding the ant to function. When you see an ant running around doing its little ant business, it seems to be working on a lone mission. The ant appears to be focused on preparing its food or building up the ant bed. The ant is the opposite from a *sluggard*, who is slow or lazy.

The rest of this section on diligence points to the consequences of laziness, which is poverty. God is helping us to see that if we choose to be lazy, we will pay a steep price for our slothfulness. When the passage says *a little sleep*, I cannot help but think back to my childhood when my mother would wake me up. I typically responded by saying, "Just five more minutes, Mom." Many people go through life all of the time looking for *just five more minutes*, and then poverty comes in *like a vagabond* or *armed man*. The picture is that of a thief who sneaks in while we are slumbering and robbing us of life and wealth.

The negative consequences of poverty are overcome by the positive outcomes of wealth. Proverbs 10:4-5 carries a similar message without the insect imagery:

> *Poor is he who works with a negligent hand,*
> *But the hand of the diligent makes rich.*

He who gathers in summer is a son who acts wisely,
  But he who sleeps in harvest is a son who acts shamefully.

Solomon emphasized the need to be *diligent*. This word not only means working hard, but it also means doing our work with enthusiasm. This admonition carries with it the same message found in Ecclesiastes 9:10, "Whatever your hand finds to do, do it with all your might." It is quite possible to work hard with a sour attitude, which does not honor God. This passage makes it clear that we are called to be enthusiastic workers.

> "We have a choice every day regarding the attitude we will embrace for that day. We cannot change our past. Nor can we change the fact that people will act in a certain way. The only thing that we can do is play on the one string we have, and that is our attitude."
>
> Charles Swindoll

Our attitude in our work reflects God's nature and ultimately brings financial gain. As we reflect upon the genre of a proverb, we recognize that this passage is not literally saying that everyone who works enthusiastically will become financially wealthy, but the principle of financial gain is certainly underscored. I cannot help but think of all of the other ways we can become rich. When we have right attitudes about our labor, we find great enjoyment in work and in life. When we look at life and work with the right perspective, we will find wealth in every area of life.

If we choose laziness when we should be working, this passage tells us we are acting *shamefully*. The imagery is that of a son bringing shame to his father or family. Think about this problem from a Christian standpoint. If we go to school and do not do our best, we are acting shamefully. If we work only thirty hours a week when we're paid to work forty, we are not representing our heavenly Father well.

Proverbs 12:24 says, "The hand of the diligent will rule," and Proverbs 22:29 states, "Do you see a man skilled in his work? He will stand before kings; He will not stand before obscure men." While the lazy person will bring reproach on his family and upon the Lord, the diligent person will be given greater responsibility in life and will ultimately become a leader.

I have always challenged my children to work hard. I told them to always be willing to go the second mile. I believe it was Roger Staubach who first said, "There are no traffic jams along the extra mile." If we work hard and engage our labor with enthusiasm, we will stand out among our fellow employees, and eventually we rise up with pay increases and promotions. We will be given not only greater responsibility, but we will also have greater opportunities to influence others. We may even *stand before kings*. Even though we do not have many kings in our culture, we have many people of great power and influence. When we work with diligence, we may find that we have the opportunity to influence the influencers of society.

When Billy Graham became a Christian in 1934 at the age of sixteen-years-old, he had no idea that he would one day stand before various presidents of the United States as spiritual adviser and friend. He is recognized as one of the greatest influential Christian leaders of modern time and must certainly be one of the noted men of American history. How did this prominence happen? It came in response to God's blessing and call on his life, but it also came in response to diligent study, prayer, and obedience to which Dr. Graham remained faithful to the very end of his life. He once reflected on aging and what we can learn through life in our twilight years, "Certainly, one lesson is to remind us of our responsibility to be diligent in our service for God right now. I may not be able to do everything I once did (nor does God expect me to), but I am called to be faithful to what I can do."[13]

A Life Out of Control

Living a life without diligence, hard work, or intentionality carries with it significant problems. Consider the words of Proverbs 25:28: "Like a city that is broken into and without walls is a man who has no control over his spirit." Working hard and living on purpose flows from the life of a person who has *control over his spirit*. This person is not just blown along through life like a leaf in our backyard on a fall afternoon. He lives every day connected to life's greater meaning. Diligence is connected to living in God's Spirit. It is no coincidence that the list of the fruit of the Spirit in Galatians 5:22-23 includes *self-control*. Laziness is born out of living in our flesh, but diligence comes from a life lived in submission to the Holy Spirit of God.

When we choose to live in our flesh without any sense of submission to God's control over our lives, we are like a *city that is broken into*. This comparison carries with it a picture of a city wall that has been breached by the enemy. We have a strong enemy who seeks daily to wreck our lives. Satan works constantly to breach the walls of your life and bring destruction. God calls us to full surrender and faithful living. He calls us to diligence and purposeful obedience. When we chose the path of diligence, we find that the walls of protection around our lives are strong, and the blessings we experience are numerous. God calls us to work hard, be enthusiastic in all things, and live daily under the control of God's Spirit in our hearts. This commitment will bring about daily spiritual victory in our lives and be a visible witness to the world of the power of the gospel in our lives.

FURTHER THOUGHT

- Would you describe the people you know or interact with every day as diligent or lazy? What evidence would you use to back your answer?
- Are you typically enthusiastic about your work?
- Have you noticed in your life that good seems to come to those who work hard? What changes would you

need to make in your life to become an enthusiastic, hard worker?

- I illustrated diligence with Billy Graham. Who represents hard work and diligence in your mind?

- How does the lack of diligence in a person's life "break down the walls" and open up that person to evil influence?

- I mentioned the fruit of the Spirit from Galatians 5:22-23. Are there any other fruits in that list that will help you be a diligent worker?

CHAPTER TEN
Don't Worry Be Happy

Do you remember Bobby McFerrin's hit song? You may not remember the artist's name, but I am quite confident you know the song, even if you weren't even born when it first came out. Here's part of the first verse:

In every life we have some trouble
But when you worry you make it double
Don't worry, be happy.

You're probably smiling by now. The song was released in September of 1988 and became the first a cappella song to reach the Billboard Hot 100 chart. So many people worry about everything that it makes us think that worry has become one of America's favorite past times. Has worry ever accomplished anything positive in your life? Corrie ten Boom once said, "Worry does not empty tomorrow of its sorrow; it empties today of its strength."

McFerrin's song said, "Don't worry; be happy." Is the opposite of worry really happiness? I'm not sure, but I do know that worry is a detriment to happiness. I cannot imagine anyone not wanting to be happy. Proverbs 10:28

says, "The hope of the righteous is gladness, but the expectation of the wicked perishes."

Is gladness your hope? Do we all wake up every morning wanting to be happy? In this verse, Solomon contrasted the *righteous* with the *wicked*. It seems that he used *hope* and *expectation* in more of a synonymous fashion. He doesn't tell us exactly what the wicked hope for or expect, but we can probably imagine. The wicked may hope for power or wealth. Maybe, they hope for sex or the material things that belong to others. Even if the wicked's dreams are fulfilled, they do not bring them happiness. How many times have we heard stories of someone gaining all of the wealth they could imagine but still being empty and miserable?

> "He who believes in the Son has eternal life; but he who does not obey the Son will not see life, but the wrath of God abides on him."
>
> John 3:36

Regardless of the expectations of those who turn their backs on God, they perish. The Bible tells us that apart from a relationship with Jesus Christ, we have no hope for eternity. Romans 6:23 reminds us that the great penalty for our sin is death. For those who reject Christ, it does not really matter what expectations they have. Those expectations will perish as the wicked slip into a Christless eternity.

What does it mean to say that the righteous *hope* for gladness? We may use the word *hope* in a different way than Solomon. I can say, "I hope that it doesn't rain tomorrow," and I am expressing a wish with no confidence that tomorrow will be dry. As a matter of fact, there's a ninety percent chance of rain tomorrow, but I'm still hoping it won't rain. We typically use the word hope to mean wishful thinking.

When God speaks of our hope in the Scripture, He does not refer to wishful thinking but rather confident expectation. Consider the message of Hebrews 11:1: "Now faith is the assurance of things hoped for, the conviction of things not seen." When Proverbs 10:28 says the hope of the righteous is gladness, the words mean that the righteous have a confident expectation that gladness will be realized in their lives.

Don't Worry Be Wise

In chapter seven, we saw where the word *blessed* means *happy* or *joyful*. When Solomon said, "How blessed is the man who finds wisdom and the man who gains understanding" (Proverbs 3:13), he was giving us a formula for happiness in our lives. Do you like formulas? I have to confess that when I was in school, I hated math. I am quite interested, however, in formulas for life. Life has many valuable formulas that work.

In the case of Proverbs 3:13, Solomon presented this formula:

Wisdom + Understanding = Happiness.

Is the path to happiness really that simple? The formula is accurate. The problem is that people do not look for wisdom and understanding in the right place. Where do people usually look for wisdom and understanding? Talk radio? Hollywood? The magazine rack at the grocery store?

We have already seen in Proverbs 9:10 that wisdom begins with fearing God. This concept is repeated again in Proverbs 15:33, "The fear of the Lord is the instruction for wisdom, and before honor comes humility." Notice the new thought this verse presents. Fearing God is the *instruction* for wisdom. When we submit to God and give Him

> "Take hold of instruction; do not let go. Guard her, for she is your life."
>
> Proverbs 4:13

the rightful place in our lives, it is like we enroll in the school of wisdom. Our classes on how to be wise have just begun.

Why do you think that in the same verse that says fearing God is the instruction for wisdom, we are also told that humility comes before honor? Remember that Hebrew poetry often expresses the same thought in two different ways or uses the second half of the couplet to expound upon the first. In this case, we see an emphasis again on fearing God. We cannot fear God with pride in our lives. If we want wisdom and the honor that comes with wisdom, we must humble ourselves before the Lord. Not only does pride keep us from fearing God, but also it keeps us from gaining wisdom. Look how Proverbs 29:23 expresses this thought:

A man's pride will bring him low, but a humble spirit will obtain honor.

Have you ever been brought low by your pride? *The Emperor's New Clothes* is a children's story that offers an excellent example of this problem. The emperor was so full of himself that he could not admit that the scoundrels who had supposedly made him the finest clothes had actually made nothing at all. It was the king's pride that kept him from admitting that the supposed tailors were swindlers. It took the honesty of a child to point out that the king was naked. His pride brought him low. We will deal with pride and humility in another chapter, but we can at this point glean that pride is a huge barrier to happiness. Pride brings us low and robs us of our joy. Humility, on the other hand, brings honor and ultimately happiness.

The Path to Happiness

We have seen that true happiness begins with wisdom, but what are some other qualities or experiences that will continually guide us down the path of joy? Proverbs 14:21 says, "He who despises his neighbor sins, but happy is he who is gracious to the poor." This proverb underscores the truth that we find happiness in community with others. In this case, our community is with the poor.

Notice the contrast of this proverb: despising your neighbor versus showing grace to the poor.

What does it mean to despise your neighbor? When we despise someone, we look down upon them with contempt or think of them as worthless and not worthy of our time or attention. Do you see the contrast of despising someone and being gracious to the poor? If you despise your neighbor, you ignore

> "You know, when you've experienced grace and you feel like you've been forgiven, you're a lot more forgiving of other people."
>
> Rick Warren

them and turn a blind eye to their needs. When God says that this kind of attitude is sin, I cannot help but think about Cain's comment to God when God asked about Able: "Am I my brother's keeper?" God's unspoken answer was, "Yes, why wouldn't you be your brother's keeper?" As part of God's family and as a member of the human race, we are all interconnected with all of humanity.

Do you remember Jesus' parable of the good Samaritan (Luke 10:25-37)? He told that story in response to a religious expert's question: "Who is my neighbor?" This religious leader may have considered a lot of people his neighbor, but Jesus' story said that a Samaritan was the neighbor of a Jew. A Samaritan never would have lived next door to a Jewish family because Jews typically hated Samaritans. In the story, it was a Samaritan man who stopped to help a Jewish person who had been hurt by thieves. The inference is that anyone and everyone could be considered our neighbor, and we are responsible to help anyone in need.

For me to ignore the needs of people around me is a sin. Not only is ignoring them a sin, but also it steals my joy. Even as showing grace to the poor brings happiness, despising our neighbor brings us sorrow. Are you wrapped up in your own goals and dreams and ignoring the needs of your neighbors? If so, you are sinning.

Another important step on the path to happiness is obedience to the Word of God. Proverbs 29:18 states, "Where there is no vision, the people are unrestrained, but happy is he who keeps the law." I have seen this verse used often to challenge Christians and particularly churches to be people of vision. Some church leaders opt to use this scripture as a theme for a ministry strategy presentation or a building campaign. I memorized the King James Version as a child, "Where there is no vision, the people perish." Is this passage really talking about developing a plan for the future? Will people really die if they do not have a well thought out plan for their lives?

The word that is translated *vision* could be translated *revelation*. This word could be used for the vision of the prophets or literally for a word from God. If you look at the complete couplet, this idea becomes more obvious. The word *vision* is paralleled with the word *law*. Let's paraphrase this proverb by using the term "word from God." It would be as if the proverb writer is saying,

"Where there is no word from God, the people are unrestrained, but happy is he who keeps God's Word."

Vision is certainly an appropriate translation, but we must connect this understanding of sight to the revealed

> "Your Word is a
> lamp to my feet
> and a light to my
> path."
>
> Psalm 119:105

truth of God. From a Christian's perspective, can we really have the right view of our goals and dreams without considering God's Word regarding our futures? This proverb underscores the importance of always seeking God's revelation about His plan for our lives. We are reminded here of the futility of sitting around and dreaming up possibilities for our future without considering God's Word. This idea means that whether you are thinking of your future as an individual or as being a part of a dream team for your church, the starting point is always the Word of God.

Other than the fact that he was inspired by God, why did the writer choose to say that people who do not have a word from God are *unrestrained?* The Hebrew word literally means to "let loose." We could even interpret this verse as to saying that people who do not have a word from God have "let their hair down." The only thing is that this concept is a negative one and not positive. We do not want to be unrestrained. It would not honor God, and it would divert us from the proper path of life.

I just saw a good example of unrestraint. I am currently on an airplane flying back to Atlanta, and I noticed the movie a woman in front of me was watching. I was stunned. I looked around to make sure no children were around who could happen to see what was on the screen on the back of the seat in front of her. Some Hollywood screen writer without a *vision* wrote a script that presented a scene where the people were totally unrestrained. I have no idea what movie she was watching, but that scene was not suitable for any person in any circumstance. The very fact that we live in a culture that accepts that movie as fitting means that we are a culture who has let loose and is unrestrained.

This concept is not portraying the idea of simply not being so rigid. I think it would help a lot of Christians to loosen up. God's Word is not intended to put us into the bondage of legalism. Some believers have been led to believe that even good, clean fun is not appropriate for Christians. Nothing could be further from the truth. This passage even says that the person who lives according to God's Word will experience great happiness.

Have you ever thought about Jesus' life on earth with His disciples? I imagine Jesus and the Twelve sitting around a campfire laughing over some of the events of the day. Do you suppose Jesus ever told a joke? If He did, you know He would have been a perfect joke teller. He would have had His friends rolling with laughter. Does it feel sacrilegious to think of the Son of God laughing with His friends? Surely, the One who said, "A joyful heart is good medicine, but a broken spirit dries up the bones" (Proverbs 17:22) would have been One who would experience a good belly laugh from time to time.

God invented happiness and designed joy for His
children. Are you happy? It is God's plan for your life.

FURTHER THOUGHT

- Do you struggle with worry? If so, have you ever
  found that worry robs you of happiness?
- Have you ever found God teaching you things about
  wisdom in response to your respect and relationship
  with Him? If so, what?
- Has pride ever brought you low? Can you think of
  how pride will be a barrier to true joy in your life?
- Do you often show grace to the poor? What if "the
  poor" means something more than just those who do
  not have money? Do you often act graciously toward
  those who are poor in character or in good decisions?
  Is there someone in your life right now who needs you
  to act in grace toward them?
- How might showing grace toward those in need bring
  happiness to your life?
- If you live an unrestrained life without a clear vision
  of God's truth, what are you willing to do to make sure
  that you live happily within God's law?

CHAPTER ELEVEN
The Joy of Generosity

I once read about a telephone survey in which a question was asked, "Do you consider yourself to be a generous person?" How do you think people responded? Ninety percent said yes. We probably shouldn't be surprised because most people want to see themselves as generous. The surveyor followed up the first question with a second question: "Describe the last time you did something that was generous." Instead of writing down answers, the caller simply started a stop watch to see how long it took the person to give a legitimate example of generosity. The average reply took twenty seconds. If it takes at least twenty seconds for us to remember our last act of generosity, then maybe we are not as generous as we like to think we are.[14]

Generosity is so important in the life of a believer. When we give, we are reflecting the heart of our Heavenly Father: "For God so loved the world that He gave..." (John 3:16). Rick Warren said, "The word *believe* is used 272 times in the Bible. God wants you to believe. The word *pray* is used 371 times in the Bible. God wants us to pray. The word *love* is used 714 times in the Bible. God wants you to learn to love. But the word *give* is used 2,162 times." God obviously wants us to be givers.

In many cases, however, greed has replaced generosity. Andrew Greely began an article in the Chicago Sun Times with these words, "The most serious spiritual problem in the country today is reckless and untrammeled greed."[15] I'm not sure I totally agree with his conclusion that greed is our most serious spiritual problem, but greed is a serious issue that leads to many destructive actions. Because of greed, the dealer sells drugs on the street and the business tycoon cheats on his taxes. Greed is the basis of human trafficking, exploitation of young athletes, sexual abuse, and unfair practices in the workplace. While it may not be *the* most serious spiritual problem, it is a huge problem in our world today.

> "Do not eat the bread of a selfish man or desire his delicacies."
>
> Proverbs 23:6

One reason that greed grows so freely like an unnoticed weed in the corner of the backyard is because it is tied to our basic nature of selfishness and self-centeredness. Selfishness is the root expression of all sin. Because we are born with a natural inclination to sin, we live our lives with ourselves sitting on the thrones of our own hearts. We want to be our own sovereign and to plan out our personal destinies. We think we are the center of our universes, and our actions and attitudes will always consider our wishes and needs first above the needs of everyone else. Selfishness and greed are like twin brothers, and they ultimately bring great sorrow to ourselves and others within our relational sphere. Proverbs 11:26 states, "He who withholds grain, the people will curse him, but blessing will be on the head of him who sells it." This passage carries the familiar theme of blessings and curses. In this case, curses come from people toward someone who is greedy and selfish. Blessings will be on those who are generous.

Our Generosity is a Blessing to Others

Proverbs 15:27 states, "Greed brings grief to the whole family" (NLT). While we think that our actions and attitudes are only our business, the Bible establishes the truth that many other people are impacted by our sins. How does greed bring grief to the whole family? Let's imagine a father who is greedy. His greed is first expressed in daily attitudes as he relates to his wife and children. His focus is upon himself, and he seeks to be served instead of being a servant. This attitude stirs contempt in the heart of his wife and trains his children to act the same way toward one another and to others in their lives.

Greed always has a payday. It expresses itself in our lives in many ways and is never satisfied with only a small piece of our hearts. Greed stirs discontentment and births materialism. It directs us to buy an eighty-inch television when our forty-inch flat screen would serve us perfectly well. Greed leads to excesses in every area of life and can ultimately lead toward alcoholism, immorality, or bankruptcy. This passage says that when greed becomes the culture of a family, the whole family is impacted by grief. It becomes a cyclical sin that is passed down to the next generation, and it destroys marriages and families as it works to eat away at our hearts.

While greed destroys, generosity builds. Generosity builds up others around us, and it builds up our own lives. One of the greatest ways to overcome the natural tendency toward greed is to become a giver. Becoming a generous giver is like throwing water on the wicked witch in the Wizard of Oz, except this time, the wicked witch is greed. As we become generous toward others, that evil fiend within our hearts begins to shrivel up. We become like the Grinch who loved Christmas. Other people around us are impacted by our generosity, and God is honored with our spirit that reflects His nature.

> "The generous man will be prosperous, and he who waters, will himself be watered."
>
> Proverbs 11:25

Proverbs 3:9 admonishes us, "Honor the Lord with your wealth, with the firstfruits of all your crops." How do you honor the Lord with your wealth? We can answer that question in a variety of ways, and they could all be true. We certainly honor God by being wise in our spending. One hundred percent of our wealth actually belongs to God, so we should understand that every financial decision we make is a spiritual decision. Christians often times want to debate what it means to give ten

percent to God in a tithe and whether or not that Old
Testament principle is meant for New Testament
believers. I can tell you on the authority of Scripture that
God is not only interested in ten percent, He is interested
in 100 percent! Honor the Lord with *all* of your wealth.

We also honor the Lord by giving a *firstfruits offering*.
The Bible teaches that the firstfruits offering points to a
tithe of ten percent. When I give a tithe of my income (an
offering of ten percent of my paycheck), I am giving the
firstfuits of my income. I know that some people say that
they don't *have* to give because that principle seems to
have more of an Old Testament focus. My thought is that
if the Old Testament followers gave ten percent because
of the law, how much more should we give because of
grace? Shouldn't love be more compelling than the law?

I know that we're not an agricultural society anymore,
so we can't give the firstfruits of our crops, but we can
give the firstfruits of our paycheck. If the people in
Malachi's day were robbing God because they refused to
give their tithes (Malachi 3:8-10), then I think we have a
lot of thieves in our day. One way our offerings through
the church are a blessing to others is that our churches are
able to bless people through ministry, missions, and
benevolence. God is honored as others are blessed.

We are admonished to be generous to others in verses
such as Proverbs 21:13: "He who shuts his ear to the cry
of the poor will also cry himself and not be answered."
God says that being generous is His nature, and He has
written it into the DNA of His followers. If we choose to

shut our ears and eyes to the needs of others around us, we, too, will one day find ourselves suffering as a result.

Our Generosity is a Blessing to Ourselves

According to an old adage, "What goes around, comes around." I am confident that our motive for giving should always be to honor the Lord and to help other people; however, God clearly says in His Word that we are also the beneficiaries of being generous to others. It is the principle of reciprocity. Consider the words of Proverbs 14:30-31:

A heart at peace gives life to the body,
but envy rots the bones.
He who oppresses the poor shows contempt for the Maker,
but whoever is kind to the needy honors God (NIV).

Because a peaceful heart gives us life, we should ponder the source of a peaceful heart. This two-verse proverb offers us a clue to the source of peace. You have to go to the second verse of the proverb to see the contrasting statement to rotting envy and oppression. The contrast is found in being kind to the needy. It is a picture of generosity. Our conclusion is that not only does it honor God and bless other people, but also it gives life to our bodies.

This passage carries a small statement that we could find on our doctor's prescription pads. Everything about our lives seems to attack our health. We know that stress and struggle lead to poor health. This verse says that a heart at peace gives life. In other words, a heart without turmoil and stress will prolong your days on this planet. The inference of the proverb is that envy robs us of peace. One way to overcome envy is to quit focusing on ourselves and our wants. Start focusing on serving other people, and you will find that envy has to flee. Start giving to the needs of other people, and peace will drive out stress.

When we are motivated by a heart of greed and oppress the poor, we show that we really do not care about God and His desires for our lives. We show contempt for our Maker. God has a heart for the poor, and so should we. Proverbs 19:17 says, "One who is gracious to a poor man lends to the Lord, and He will repay him for his good deed." The Hebrew word that is translated as *poor* can mean *feeble*, *weak*, or *helpless*. This state of helplessness could come from financial problems, but it could also encompass a number of other issues that leads someone to a state of helplessness. The bottom line is that God calls us to be gracious toward people who are unable to help themselves.

> "He who despises his neighbor sins, but happy is he who is gracious to the poor."
>
> Proverbs 14:21

We should not read this verse as if we are lending something to God because He stands in need. What does the writer mean when he says that when we act graciously toward the poor, we are lending to the Lord? One commentary expressed the following: "To be compassionate to the poor is figuratively to put God in your debt."[16] The idea of putting God in our debt feels a little sacrilegious to me because I will forever be in debt to Him. God does establish the truth, however, that when we embrace those who are poor or needy, we are embracing Christ. We see this concept mentioned in the words of Jesus in Matthew 25:40: "Truly, I say to you, to the extent that you did it to one of these brothers of Mine, even the least of them, you did it to Me."

The focus of lending to the Lord is not on us giving something Jesus needs, but rather Jesus paying us back with interest. When we borrow money from the bank to purchase a home, we pay the principle back plus interest. God is saying that whenever we serve those who cannot serve themselves, He will reward our faithfulness. For this reason, the second part of this couplet says God will *repay him for his good deed*. The payment is more than just whatever was paid out. Have you ever gone to minister to someone through a visit and left feeling as if you were the one served? God rewards us in a variety of different ways, but whenever we obey Him and serve others, we will always benefit. This principle is repeated in Proverbs 11:25, "The generous man will be prosperous, and he who waters will himself be watered."

Do you want to live your lives being a blessing to God? Be a blessing to others. Live generously with open hands. Hands that are open not only give to bless others, but they also receive God's blessings in return.

FURTHER THOUGHT

- Are you a generous person? When was the last time you did something generous? What was it?

- Have you ever seen greed bring grief to a whole family? Write down a list of things that can happen to a family as a result of greed. What steps will you take to guard your family against greed?

- As stated in this chapter, one of the best ways to overcome greed is to be a giver. Are you a giver? If not, are you willing to become one?

- Do you honor the Lord with your wealth? Do you tithe? Do you give in other ways beyond financially? How can you improve in this area?

- What are some specific ways you are willing to be gracious to the poor? Can you think of a ministry project you can do with a small group of Christian friends?

CHAPTER TWELVE

Avoiding the Cost of Money

"You can't live with it, and you can't live without it."
This idiom is often applied to a variety of different
subjects: sports, men (or women), computers, or cell
phones. In the Bible, and particularly in the book of
Proverbs, the subject could be money. The fact is that you
have to own some money to survive, but the problem
often arises that we allow money to own us. Although we
know that balance is important, we may find it easier to
walk across the Grand Canyon on a tightrope than to
maintain a proper balance with money.

I have been a pastor for many years, and I know that
people get a little nervous when the topic switches to
money. Many folks think that money is the only thing
preachers think about.

I love the story of two men who were stranded on an
island with no food or water. One of the men kept running around saying, "We're going to die! We're going to
die!" while the other one simply sat calmly on the beach
under a palm tree.

The guy that was upset finally ran up to the other man
and said, "How can you just sit here like nothing's hap-
pening. Don't you realize that we don't have any food or
water, and we're stranded on this island?"

The man just smiled at his frantic friend. "Sure. I realize that, but I make $20,000 per week."

"Who cares how much money you make," the friend screamed, waving his arms in the air. "That means absolutely nothing to us out here in the middle of nowhere."

"On the contrary. You see, I'm a Christian, and I'm very active in my church. I give ten percent of my income to my church. My pastor will find me."

Although it is true that some pastors may have impure motives in regard to money, most of us just want the Church to be obedient, and we want to teach the Word of God faithfully. Jesus spent more time talking about money or wealth than any other topic. Think for a moment about that statement. Jesus talked more about money than He did Heaven or Hell and many other topics. Consider these biblical facts:

- Over 2000 passages in the Bible deal with money or wealth.
- Approximately two-thirds of Jesus' parables make some reference to money.
- There are more verses related to giving than any other subject on money.

These truths emphasize the fact that if preachers did not try to help their congregations understand how to earn, manage, spend, invest, and give money, then they would not be faithfully teaching the entire Word of God. To ignore this topic is to not be true to our calling.

God offers us some help with this issue of money in the book of Proverbs. In looking at this topic or any other topic that is addressed in Proverbs, we must realize that God is not giving us every lesson we need to learn in regard to that particular issue. It is best to study the entire Bible with a particular topic in mind to ascertain God's full teaching on the matter. We can learn some important principles about money, however, by looking at the various scriptures in this book of wisdom.

A Proper Perspective

When it comes to the issue of money, it is easy to not only get out of balance, but also to lose perspective. One thing about money is that we all need it, and we probably all think we need a little more than we have. Proverbs 15:16-17 helps us to have a proper view of our finances:

Better is a little with the fear of the Lord
Than great treasure and turmoil with it.
Better is a dish of vegetables where love is
Than a fattened ox served with hatred.

The obvious contrast of this passage is a little bit of money versus a lot of money. The writer points out that there are a lot of things in life that are worse than being broke. Remember that wisdom starts with the *fear of the Lord*, so it should be no surprise to us that as long as we have the *fear of the Lord*, being bereft of material things is not so bad. This passage hints to other truths that the Bible presents: great treasure can also bring a lot of problems. Verse sixteen says that great treasure can bring *turmoil.* Other places in the Bible translate that word as confusion (Deuteronomy 7:23), disturbances (2 Chronicles 15:5), or panic (Isaiah. 22:5). These are all experiences one might encounter in response to having great treasure.

It is easy to see how having a lot of money could bring about confusion and panic. I have heard lottery winners say that winning a lot of money was the worse day of their lives. Time Magazine even published an article a couple of years ago entitled, "Here's How Winning the Lottery Makes You Miserable." If we're not careful, having a lot of money can cause us not to see life from a proper perspective.

What is the idea that is held in highest regard in this passage? Once again, it is the fear of the Lord. Do you want confusion, turmoil, or panic, or would you rather have the fear of the Lord? It is far better to be in proper relationship with God and have nothing than to have everything you can imagine but be far from the Lord. It is interesting that the writer said vegetables and love

> "Progress will only bring us increasing pain. Our wallets will get fatter, our houses bigger, our cars faster, and our brains smarter. Yet when we neglect the most important priorities, our final reward will fittingly be all the unhappiness money can buy."
>
> Richard Swenson

are better than steak and hate. It is so easy for us to think that money is the most important thing and great wealth would solve all of our problems. That perspective is the lie that Satan feeds us every day.

Before we consider some negative aspects of money, I must state that God is not against wealth. A number of the Proverbs, like Proverbs 10:4, challenge us to work hard and make money, "Poor is he who works with a negligent hand, but the hand of the diligent makes rich." It is not evil to be wealthy. The biblical principles regarding wealth includes being a good steward of our financial resources so we can be givers and bless other people and to make sure that we are not allowing money to become our god. We also have numerous scriptural warnings not to earn money in unethical ways. Some people, however, even have gifts of giving (Rom 12:8), and if you have a gift of giving, you will probably have the means to give as well.

The Problem with Wealth

Proverbs 11:28 offers another contrasting perspective: "He who trusts in his riches will fall, but the righteous will flourish like the green leaf." In comparing trusting in riches and being righteous, we will either fall or flourish. Compare this proverb with the one mentioned above, Proverbs 15:16-17. The two verses in Proverbs 15 make an emphatic statement that great treasure *will* bring great turmoil or trouble. Proverbs 11:28 focuses on the problem of trusting in riches and says that the one who trusts in riches *will* fall. Maybe these two texts should be read together. Possibly one reason great treasure will bring great turmoil is because material wealth can easily lead to independence instead of God dependence. This proverb also contrasts the righteous with those who trust in riches. This passage makes me think of Jesus' words in Matthew 6:24 where He told us that no one can serve two masters. If you trust in riches, you cannot trust in God.

Choosing to place your faith in Christ leads you to *flourish like a green leaf.* Isn't it interesting that we typically think we will flourish if we have great wealth? Satan has led us to believe that money will solve all of our problems, but God says loving money is the root of all evil (1 Tim 6:10). If we choose to trust in the Lord and not riches, we will flourish. What do you suppose that concept means? What comes to your mind when you think of the word *flourish?* I think of healthy, green plants or lush mountain forests. When I think of flourishing, I think of something that is growing and healthy. I think of something producing fruit and being a blessing to others. The Hebrew word used in that passage means to bud or sprout, and by inference, it means to thrive.

> "He will be like a tree firmly planted by streams of water, which yields its fruit in its season and its leaf does not wither; and in whatever he does, he prospers."
>
> Psalm 1:3

I want to thrive! I'm sure you do, too. We will thrive if we trust in the Lord and live in surrender to Jesus Christ.

Proverbs 18:11 gives additional insight to a problem with wealth: "A rich man's wealth is his strong city, and like a high wall in his own imagination." If this verse stopped after the first half, we might think it is a passage telling us that wealth will offer us great protection. The second half of the couplet, however, informs us that the rich man's protection is actually an illusion. His wealth is like a high wall in his *own imagination*. We know that wealth can provide many things in life, including a great security system in our homes, but money can never provide us full proof protection. I like how the Psalmist expressed this in Psalm 20:7, "Some boast in chariots and some in horses, but we will boast in the name of the Lord, our God."

The Last Word

A summary statement of God's perspective on money must include a challenge to work hard, make money, provide for your family, and bless others. At the same time, verses like Proverbs 23:4-5 remind us that chasing wealth is an unproductive, exhausting enterprise:

> *Do not weary yourself to gain wealth,*
> *Cease from your consideration of it.*
> *When you set your eyes on it, it is gone.*
> *For wealth certainly makes itself wings*
> *Like an eagle that flies toward the heavens.*

We must be careful not to allow something to take the place of God in our lives. The first commandment reminds us to always keep God first. When money becomes our god, we are never satisfied, and while we may have a lot of money at one moment, it can be gone the next. If you don't believe that, just ask a few investors to tell you about their portfolios in 2008 through 2012. Wealth can indeed make itself wings and fly away. Regardless of whether you are wealthy or just earn enough money to make ends meet, we should always make sure that God is the One who sits on the throne of our hearts and that we always use our financial resources in a way that honors the Lord.

FURTHER THOUGHT

- Does it bother you to hear pastors preach about money? Why? What is your reaction to the truth that Jesus spoke more about wealth than any other topic?

- Have you ever experience turmoil because of wealth in your life? What led to your trouble, and what did you do to overcome it?

- Do you fear the Lord? If you were on trial for fearing the Lord, what evidence would the prosecuting attorney use to try to convict you?

- Make a brief list of ways that you think the righteous may flourish like a green leaf. Have you ever experienced any of these things in your life? What are some steps you could take now to experience this kind of personal growth?

- Do you weary yourself to gain wealth? How can you put the pursuit of wealth into a proper perspective in your life?

CHAPTER THIRTEEN
The First Duty of Society – Justice

"…With liberty and justice for all." How many times have we said those words? If you are a citizen of the United States, I dare say that you have repeated them hundreds of times because they are the concluding words of the Pledge of Allegiance. Alexander Hamilton said, "I think the first duty of society is justice."

The word *justice* is used many times in foundational documents of the United States. Regardless of the country which you call home, we often hear of justice, but is true justice a possibility in our time?

A cursory search on the Internet of the word *justice* reveals that it means being just or right. A number of dictionaries may point to moral rightness. We often times equate the word *fairness* with justice. I have always heard that life is not fair, but does that mean that *we* should not work to treat others fairly? What about the Golden Rule? Jesus said in Matthew 7:12, "In everything, therefore, treat people the same way you want them to treat you, for this is the Law and the Prophets." Look again at the last few words of the Golden Rule: *for this is the Law and the Prophets*. Wow! Jesus is saying that this statement about the way we treat others summarizes what the early church, before the New Testament was written, knew to be the Bible.

God inspired the writers of Proverbs to underscore the importance of acting justly toward others. Consider the words of Proverbs 21:3: "To do righteousness and justice is desired by the Lord more than sacrifice." Keep in mind that this verse was written to a people who were steeped in the practice of sacrifice. The Jews' entire calendar revolved around festivals that centered on sacrifices. God commanded them in the Old Testament scriptures to make sacrifices for their sins. It is with that backdrop that we read that acting righteously and with justice is more desirable than sacrifice. Why would God say make that statement? It seems to contradict the Old Testament scripture.

This passage first elevates the importance of justice. Even as God put a high priority on the sacrificial system, He is emphasizing the significance of always acting right and justly in relationship with other people.

> "Has the LORD as much delight in burnt offerings and sacrifices as in obeying the voice of the LORD? Behold, to obey is better than sacrifice, and to heed than the fat of rams."
>
> I Samuel 15:22

The second thing Proverbs 21:3 insinuates, especially when considered in light of passages such as Isaiah 1, is that it is possible to follow the sacrificial system perfectly and still be far from God. Isaiah chastised Israel with these words from the Lord: "I have had enough of burnt offerings of rams and the fat of fed cattle, and I take no pleasure in the blood of bulls, lambs, or goats" (Isa. 1:11). Isn't it interesting that God was saying that He had had enough of the sacrifices He commanded them to make? He was not disgusted as much with their sacrifices as He was with their motives behind the sacrifice. This same attitude is why God led Samuel to say to King Saul, "To obey is better than sacrifice" (1 Sam. 15:22).

Although the Israelites did the right things on the outside, their hearts were far from God; however, God is more concerned with character than conduct. It feels a little odd to say that God is not as concerned with our conduct. Didn't He give us the Ten Commandments?

It is possible to jump through religious hoops and still have a heart that is dark with sin. The reality is that when our character is right, our conduct will also be right. But, just because our conduct is right in the eyes of people around us does not mean that our hearts are right in the eyes of God who really knows us. Based upon Proverbs 21:3, acting righteously and with justice is a high priority to our Creator.

Challenges to Justice in our Society

The marketplace has not changed much since Solomon's time. Although we no longer use scales to determine the price of merchandise in the same way merchants did in ancient Israel, we still see the same kind of greed and deceitfulness in sales practices around the world. If you want to know about the integrity of the marketplace, just analyze some commercials on television. Seth Godin even wrote a book entitled "All Marketers Are Liars." The sales page for Godin's book emphasizes, "Great marketers don't talk about features or even benefits. Instead, they tell a story—a story we want to believe, whether it's factual or not." For example, I just read about an advertisement today that promised a hand-held, laser device would safely treat more than 200 diseases, including cancer. Fox News reported, "A former dentist-turned-con man and his two cohorts were sentenced to prison on Friday for their roles in a multi-million-dollar fraud case that primarily preyed on the elderly."[17]

What is the core challenge to people to be just? I mentioned *greed* and *deceitfulness* in the previous paragraph. Is that the problem? Proverbs 17:23 give us the answer: "The wicked accepts a bribe in secret to pervert the ways of justice" (ESV). The challenge to justice in our society today is wickedness. Before you write off wickedness as only being the problem of serial killers and child molesters, let's remind ourselves of the words of Jeremiah 17:9, "The heart is more deceitful than all else and is desperately sick; who can understand it?" Our society says, "Trust your heart," but God says, "Trust the Lord with all of your heart."

> "The way of the wicked is like darkness; they do not know over what they stumble."
>
> Proverbs 4:19

This injustice is seen in all realms of our society. The poor are mistreated. Some entrepreneurs take advantage of the gullible. Political systems sometimes favor a certain class. All of us have probably watched court cases unfold and wondered whether or not justice was served. Wickedness is evident everywhere we turn.

Before we get too upset over all of those deceitful advertisers and high-powered lawyers, let's remind ourselves of the words of that old spiritual, "It's me, it's me, it's me O Lord, standing in the need of prayer." The base evil in the heart of all of humanity is the greatest challenge to justice, and we were all born sinners. This statement means that we are all capable of acting unjustly toward someone. However, I have great news; there is a cure.

Justice Begins in the Heart

Proverbs 16:11 states, "A just balance and scales belong to the Lord; all the weights of the bag are His concern." This verse brings to mind a market place where merchants are weighing out purchases on a scale and charging accordingly. In the days of Jewish monarchs, it was not uncommon for a shop owner to cheat his customer by having weights that were a little heavier than advertised. King Solomon told us that a just balance belonged to the Lord. God is concerned about justice in the marketplace and justice in society. Unfortunately, scales that benefited the shop owner were just as normal in Bible times as dishonest business people are today. As you consider dishonesty in the market place, the problem is really not with mechanisms, such as scales or computer programs. The problem is with the hearts of humanity.

Jesus taught us in Luke 6:45 that you can learn a lot about people's hearts by the things they say and do: "The good man out of the good treasure of his heart brings forth what is good; and the evil man out of the evil treasure brings forth what is evil; for his mouth speaks from that which fills his heart." What is the source of the *good treasure* Jesus spoke about that is in a good man's heart? It is the Lord!

Since God is the One who changes our hearts, it makes sense for the proverb writer to say that a just balance belongs to the Lord. Even as God is the source of the good treasure of our hearts, part of that good treasure is justice. Being just and fair is not a human invention; instead, it first flows from the character of God. The reason that it is right to act justly toward others is because justice is connected to the nature of God, and God's nature defines what is true and right.

Humanity by nature is not just and fair. We naturally elevate ourselves over other people, even if it means acting unjustly toward someone else. We practice this behavior because we are born sinners. At the core of all sin is self, and selfishness and justice cannot coexist. Justice flows from a heart that is yielded to God, while selfishness and injustice are natural derivatives of a heart that is far from God. The Bible is clear that even the nature of humanity naturally takes us on a path away from justice. Proverbs 28:5 states, "Evil men do not understand justice, but those who seek the Lord understand all things." This path away from justice ultimately leads to destruction, but God has different plans for us.

God is in the heart change business. When we surrender our lives to the Lord Jesus, the Bible says that God begins a work of transformation in our lives, and one area in which this transformation is seen most profoundly is in the way we treat other people. A business man or woman who was once callous and hateful becomes sensitive and caring through the love of Jesus. A

> *Nothing expresses the love of Christ that is in us any more than the way we treat other people.*

judge who once took bribes for favorable judgments becomes the fairest of arbitrators in the courthouse. Justice flows from the heart of God through the lives of His people. Have you ever seen God radically change someone's life?

When I first met Charles, he was cleaning his gun. His wife had come to visit the church I pastored, so I dropped by on Monday night to talk with her about the Lord and invite her back. I also wanted to meet her husband, but he didn't want to meet me. He would not come into the living room to talk but rather sat in the other room putting off vibes that he desperately wanted the preacher to leave. I could see Charles clearly through the open door, and one thing was for certain: I was not welcome. Charles was a tough man. He owned a trailer park and dealt with a lot of rough people. Some might even say that he was a mean man. A year or two later, I had the wonderful privilege of leading Charles to faith in Jesus Christ, and I saw the most wonderful transformation of a once hardened heart. Charles became a part of our disaster relief team and has served Jesus all over the world during times of great difficulty. A man who was once feared by others and living for himself had become one of the most giving and loving men I know. God can change the hardest heart into a heart of compassion.

The Blessings of the Just

"What goes around, comes around." If we all live long enough, we will eventually see a boomerang affect with justice. Numbers 32:23 states, "Be sure your sin will find you out." Many people think they can get away with treating people badly, but eventually, payday comes around for everyone. One way that integrity brings blessing is in the lives of our family members. Proverbs 20:7 states, "A righteous man who walks in his integrity—How blessed are his sons after him." I want my children to be blessed, and the Bible clearly teaches that my children will reap the consequences of my behavior and character. "The apple doesn't fall far from the tree" is not just a cute saying. It is a reality. Our children become like us. Of course, our children have a free will and sometimes choose to walk in disobedience, but generally, if we walk in integrity and treat people justly, our children will learn from our actions. The benefits we enjoy from being people who act justly toward others will also be enjoyed by our children.

Proverbs 24:23-25 has the feel of something that could be said to a crooked judge about letting someone go who deserved condemnation, but the principle can be applied in a lot of circumstances:

These also are sayings of the wise.
 To show partiality in judgment is not good.
He who says to the wicked, "you are righteous,"
 Peoples will curse him, nations will abhor him
But to those who rebuke the wicked will be delight,
 And a good blessing will come upon them.

Whether you show unfair partiality in the courtroom, in the office, or on the ball field, the consequences are never good. This proverb says that these people will be cursed by others. On the international stage, it says that even nations will abhor him (a strong word for our political leaders). Look at the flip side of this proverb. If we rebuke the wicked, we will find *delight*. We will experience a *good blessing* in our lives.

In a time where many in our world struggle to walk in justice, God calls His people to come out from the world and live differently. One way we can shine the light of Jesus Christ in a very dark world is to always treat others the way we want to be treated. Through our just actions, we can reflect the heart of a just God.

FURTHER THOUGHT

- What comes to your mind when you hear the word *justice*? Do you think we live in a world where justice is enjoyed by all?

- Why do you think God would say that He wants justice more than sacrifice? Consider Proverbs 21:3: "To do righteousness and justice is desired by the Lord more than sacrifice." How would you translate this message to your life?

- What do you think are the great challenges or obstacles to justice in our society? What part does sin play?

- What is your reaction to people who take advantage of other people? Is there anything you can do to right the wrongs of others?

- Here's a list of modern-day practices where people are treated unjustly: human trafficking, abortion, poverty, unfair laws or lopsided politics, and prejudice/racism. Can you add any more to the list? Pick one of those situations or practices that you will add to your prayer list and look for ways to help turn that situation around to be something that would honor God.

CHAPTER FOURTEEN
Overflowing with Mercy

"Sweet mercy is nobility's true badge." Shakespeare had one of the characters in Titus Andronicus make that declaration, but is it actually true? I've never met anyone in nobility, so I can't really say, but I do know that this statement is supposed to be true of Christians. Sweet mercy is Christianity's true badge! In this chapter, I want us to think for a bit about this important concept. It is important because it is foundational to our own faith and relationship with Jesus. It is also important because it is the quality God uses to describe how we should act toward others.

Proverbs 3:3 states, "Let not mercy and truth forsake thee: bind them about thy neck; write them upon the table of thine heart" (KJV). I mentioned this proverb in Chapter Seven and pointed out that the Hebrew word for mercy (KJV) or kindness (NASV) is *hesed*. Although a couple of other Hebrew words may be translated as mercy, *hesed* is the most common. This word is used to describe God's mercy or kindness toward us. It is a word that emphasizes a loyalty that perseveres.

Another word that is translated as mercy by some Bible translators is the word *racham*. It means to show pity, compassion, or mercy toward someone. This word is

connected to the name God told Hosea to give his daughter, Lo-ruhamah, which means no compassion (Ho.1:6).
God made a prophetic statement through this child's
name that He would show no mercy and bring judgment
upon Israel. Lamentations 3:22 contains both of these
Hebrew words. It could have been translated, "The mercy
of the Lord never ceases, and His mercies never come to
an end." The first "mercy" is *hesed*, which led the NASV
translators to opt for the word *lovingkindnesses*. The second
"mercy" is *racham*, and these same translators chose the
word *compassions* to translate that term: "The Lord's
lovingkindnesses indeed never cease, for His compassions
never fail."

> "Blessed are the merciful, for they shall receive mercy."
> Matthew 5:7

We are told in the early verses of
Proverbs that we must not let mercy
or kindness leave us. It should always be an expression of our character, and therefore, our actions. It
makes sense that Christians should
reflect the character of God in all
that we do, and mercy is one of the
awesome qualities of our Heavenly Father. As the New
Living Translation renders it, "Never let loyalty and
kindness leave you!" This is a command for God's children and an exhortation to all of humanity.

As soon as those words slipped from my mind, I had
to hit pause in my brain. I do not want this chapter to
challenge Christians to work harder at showing mercy,
though God certainly knows that Christians somehow

forget to always where the badge of sweet mercy. There is more to living out this truth than just putting forth a greater effort.

John MacArthur said, "We are not meant to control our Christianity. Our Christianity is meant to control us. Living as a Christian means there is to be no veneer, no facade. Christianity is something that happens to us at the very center of our being, and from there, it flows out to the activities of life."[18] How does Christianity flow out from the center of your being to the activities of your life? We should really ponder this because an authentic faith *does* impact the way we live. I have thought for many years that the evidence of an authentic faith is a changed life. If there is no change, then there is no authentic faith.

Proverbs 16:6 concludes with these words, "By the fear of the Lord one keeps away from evil." Once again, we return to the idea of fearing the Lord as the foundation of right living. When we walk in a right relationship with God and properly respect Him as our Sovereign, we avoid evil in our lives. Evil shows up in so many different ways in the lives of people, and one obvious way is in how we act toward other people. I stress this concept first because I do not want just to encourage us to change our behavior. God would first want to change our hearts. As Martin Lloyd Jones said, "A Christian *is* something before he *does* something."[19] I hope this chapter will challenge all of us to evaluate our relationships with God. If our lives are not defined by sweet mercy, then may we first fall on our faces before God in repentance. Let's start with full surrender to Christ and then pursue acting with mercy toward others.

What is Mercy?

I mentioned above that mercy is both *hesed* (steadfast love) and *racham* (compassion and pity), but what does this really mean in your life? Proverbs 3:3 says that we are to bind mercy around our necks and write it upon our hearts. This quality is so important that it is to become a permanent part of our lives and disposition. Tying it around our necks indicates that it is to be constantly dangling in front of us as a reminder that we should always act with compassion, kindness, and pity toward others. It is to be written on our hearts because it should become a part of our own DNA and ooze from our actions with every beat of our hearts.

Compassion, kindness, and pity—the meanings of these words are obvious, but how do you flesh that out in daily living? Proverbs 14:21 helps us understand the application a little: "He who despises his neighbor sins, but happy is he who is gracious to the poor." Do you remember when I said there were three Hebrew words that could be translated as "mercy." Well, this verse presents the third option: *chanan*. It means to show grace or compassion. Remember the idea behind the genre of a proverb. You can understand word meanings by finding the contrasting word or supporting word within the couplet. Look at the contrast of this verse: despising your neighbor versus being gracious to the poor. To despise your neighbor means to look at them with contempt. The NLT uses the word *belittle*. Showing mercy would then mean not belittling or showing contempt toward your neighbor. It would mean to act with grace toward them, whether they deserve it or not. Grace, by the nature of its definition, has nothing to do with the status or worthiness of the recipient and everything to do with the compassion and initiative of the giver.

God is gracious toward us. Romans 3:24 jumps right into an inspired, flowing thought of the Apostle Paul: "Being justified as a gift by His grace through the redemption which is in Christ Jesus." Where would we be without the grace of God? In Hell! Throughout the Bible, and specifically in Proverbs, we are admonished to show this same grace to others.

Blessed Are the Merciful

Jesus included mercy in His list of Beatitudes when He said, "Blessed are the merciful, for they shall receive mercy." The word *blessed* means the same thing in Hebrew as it does in Greek. You could translate it as "Oh how happy" or "How full of joy are the merciful." God says that people who show mercy toward others find an inner joy and happiness. An old Chinese saying supports this truth: "If you want happiness for an hour, take a nap. If you want happiness for a day, go fishing. If you want happiness for a year, inherit a fortune. If you want happiness for a lifetime, help somebody." Blessed are the merciful!

We are always the recipients of blessing from our own acts of mercy. Proverbs 11:17 states, "The merciful man does himself good, but the cruel man does himself harm." Our motive should never be to receive anything from our acts of mercy for then it may cease to be an act of mercy. When we act out of a heart to serve others, we always walk away blessed. Jenny Santi wrote an article in *Time Magazine* entitled "The Secret to Happiness is Helping Others." In the article, she shared this interesting discovery:

> Scientific research provides compelling data to support the anecdotal evidence that giving is a powerful pathway to personal growth and lasting happiness. Through fMRI technology, we now know that giving activates the same parts of the brain that are stimulated by food and sex. Experiments show evidence that altruism is hardwired in the brain—and it's pleasurable. Helping others may just be the secret to living a life that is not only happier but also healthier, wealthier, more productive, and meaningful.[20]

Isn't that research fascinating? In God's creative mind, He wired serving others together with food and sex. At least, all of these activities share the same piece of our brains. Being merciful to other people makes us happy!

We looked at the second part of Proverbs 16:6 earlier. Let's look at the entire proverb to learn of another blessing of being merciful. "By lovingkindness and truth iniquity is atoned for, and by the fear of the Lord, one keeps away from evil." First, let's clear up something that could be a stumbling block. If Proverbs 16:6 were the only Bible verse you have ever read, you could assume that the way we gain forgiveness for our sins is through performing acts of mercy. Through reading other passages in the Bible, you know that interpretation cannot be true. Consider Titus 3:5, "He saved us, not on the basis of deeds which we have done in righteousness, but according to His mercy, by the washing of regeneration and renewing by the Holy Spirit," and a myriad of other passages, such as Ephesians 2:8-9, Romans 3:20-30, and 2 Timothy 1:9. Because God's Word cannot contradict itself, Proverbs 16:6 must point to something else.

> "A new commandment I give to you, that you love one another, even as I have loved you, that you also love one another. By this all men will know that you are My disciples, if you have love for one another."
>
> John 13:34-35

We can understand this passage's meaning from two different perspectives. First, connect it to the thought of James 2:14-17. James does not deny that salvation is by grace through faith, but he underscores that a salvation that is by grace will always show itself in works. While God led the Apostle Paul to focus on the root of salvation, which is grace, God led James to focus on the fruit of salvation, which is works. When we combine all of

Scripture, we understand that Proverbs 16:6 must indicate that iniquity is atoned for by grace that shows itself in lovingkindness and truth.

We can also connect an understanding of this passage to the focus of relationships with other people and not our relationship with God. We have all had broken relationships with other people. When we act with mercy and truth toward a friend and family member with whom we were once at odds, our relationship can be healed. The blessing of Proverbs 16:6 is that in response to God's mercy in our lives, we have atonement for our sins, and because of God's mercy, we can then act mercifully toward others. Our acts of mercy toward others can then bring unity between us and the one with whom we may be divided.

Proverbs 14:31 shows us still another blessing of the merciful: "He who oppresses the poor taunts his Maker, but he who is gracious to the needy honors Him." When we are gracious or merciful toward the needy, God is honored. When we do not act mercifully toward those in need, we taunt God. To taunt God means that we insult Him or act with contempt toward Him. The positive side of this proverb is that when we show kindness toward others, we bring glory to the name of our God.

Do you want to find happiness and fulfillment in your life? Do you want to glorify the name of Jesus who died to redeem you from your sin? Give your life to serve others. Tie mercy around your neck and write it on your heart so that every act of your life toward others will always reflect the mercy of God.

FURTHER THOUGHT

- Think for a moment about how you have personally experienced the *hesed* lovingkindness and mercy of God. Make a list of a few things God has done for you that is an expression of His mercy.

- How can you bind mercy around your neck and write it on your heart?

- How does the fear of the Lord keep you away from evil?

- How does being gracious to the poor help you to be happy? List a few ways you have shown mercy to someone who is poor.

- How has being merciful in the past been a personal blessing to you?

- Why do you think it taunts God for us to oppress the poor? Make a list of a few ways you plan to honor God by showing mercy toward others.

CHAPTER FIFTEEN
Controlling Anger Before It Controls You

I recently saw a video about road rage someone posted on Facebook. I'm not sure what precipitated the confrontation, but an older man got out of his car at a traffic light to offer the driver behind him a few words. Once he returned to his vehicle, the other guy had evidently had a little more time to become sufficiently steamed, so he drove up beside the older man and tried to ram his car. The younger guy, however, didn't just ram his agitator. Somehow, maybe the size of his tires or the angle of his car, the car rode partially up the side of the older man's vehicle and turned over on its side.

I'm not sure which depicts our times better: the rage that led a man to turn his car over or the person behind the whole scene who decided to video the confrontation. Regardless, we are finding an increase in anger behind the wheel. A study released by the AAA Foundation for Traffic Safety reported that nearly eight out of ten drivers demonstrated significant anger, aggression, or road rage in the past year.[21] Eight out of ten people is a lot of people. What is the source of this anger? What should we do when we find anger swelling up inside of us? God addressed this issue in Proverbs.

Is Anger Bad?

It seems like anger should be bad. When Paul gave a list of things to be put aside in Colossians 3:8, anger was the first vice he mentioned. As soon as those thoughts form in my mind, I suddenly have a picture of Jesus clearing the temple with a whip in His hand. Is it possible that anger is neither good or bad? The Bible even speaks of God as being angry: "God is a righteous judge and a God who has indignation every day" (Psalm 7:11). Because Jesus seemed angry when He cleansed the temple and because God has indignation every day, anger must be considered amoral. There is a difference between the car-tipping anger in the Facebook video and the table-turning anger of Jesus in the temple. The Bible points to the fact that sometimes the source of anger is sin, but other times, the source of anger is righteousness.

Going back to the temple scene, Jesus became angry because evil men were using God's house as a den of thieves. Crooks were cheating people out of money and committing numerous other acts of injustice. Luke recorded Christ's comments after clearing the temple: "It is written, 'And My house shall be a house of prayer,' but you have made it a robbers' den" (Luke 19:46).

> "Biblically, anger is God-given energy intended to help us solve problems."
>
> Gotquestions.org

One must consider two key issues when evaluating anger. The first issue has to do with motive. Why are you angry? What is the source of your anger? We might wonder about a Christian who can look at some of the evil things going on in our world and not be angry. We should be angry over the fact that more than forty million men, women, and children suffer the exploitation of human trafficking and modern-day slavery. The reality that 219 out of every 1000 births are aborted in the United States each year should make our blood boil.[22] I could probably generate quite a list of things that should cause our anger Richter scale to top out. Some of that anger might not only be justified but also be proper.

A second consideration has to do with what we do with the anger that we have? Ephesians 4:26-27 indicates that anger may be normal at times, but the problem comes in not dealing with it properly: "Be angry and yet do not sin; do not let the sun go down on your anger, and do not give the devil an opportunity." This verse will be a good one to keep in mind as we see what Proverbs has to say about anger. If we succumb to the evil side of anger, we will find that we are giving the devil an opportunity. An opportunity to do what? We would give him an opportunity to hurt our testimonies, to damage our relationships, and to fill our minds with regret. Unresolved anger can stunt our spiritual growth, restrict our ministry outreach, hurt our marriages, and scar our children.

> "A fool always loses his temper, but a wise man holds it back."
>
> Proverbs 29:11

Is anger bad? Not necessarily. The writers of Proverbs offer us a God-inspired perspective on this normal, human expression.

Anger Under Control

Is it possible for anger to start out as a normal, human reaction to a circumstance that is neither right nor wrong but move into an expression that is not God-honoring? I have no doubt that the answer is yes. Is it also equally as possible for anger to begin in our hearts as a sinful reaction to our circumstance only to be harnessed through the power of God's Spirit in our lives? Yes on both counts. Whether the source of anger is sin or righteous indignation, we are taught in Proverbs to always master it. Proverbs 12:16 states, "A fool's anger is known at once, but a prudent man conceals dishonor." Notice the contrasts of this proverb. The first character is a fool and the other is a prudent man. While the Hebrew word that was translated as *prudent* means sensible, clever, or shrewd, the writer is contrasting the concept of a *fool* with one who is wise. Notice that this verse says the foolish person's anger is known at once. This picture is of a person out of control. You know right off about this person's anger or frustration. The *prudent* man is the contrast to the foolish man, and he *conceals dishonor.*

I do not believe that God is calling us to hide our sin. Other passages point to the fact that confessing our sins to one another is a healthy practice (James 5:16), so the message of this proverb is not to hide sinful anger.

Instead, this scripture emphasizes the importance of self-control. Foolish people explode without control, and the fallout from these explosions can be devastating. A wise person has learned the discipline of self-control and, therefore, carefully and obediently deals with his anger. When righteous anger should be expressed, the wise person does so in a way that honors the Lord.

Proverbs 14:29 carries a similar message: "He who is slow to anger has great understanding, but he who is quick-tempered exalts folly." We use a variety of words and expressions for people who are patient. We might say they are long-fused, forbearing, long-suffering, or easy going. In the original Hebrew of this passage, the writer literally said, "Long in nostrils, great in understanding." Long nostrils doesn't communicate anything to us today, but 3000 years ago, it meant being very slow to become angry. God is saying that people who have control of their emotions and do not react quickly in anger have great understanding. My mind paused on this nugget and asked, "Understanding of what?" You can fill in the blank with various answers.

When we are slow to become angry in a situation, we first have a great understanding of God and His Kingdom. We are able to look at our circumstances through God's eyes and gain an eternal perspective. From this type of understanding, we may see the futility of becoming emotional or passionate about a particular event because we realize that in the long run, it really doesn't matter.

We can also be slow to anger when we understand people. It is a fact that hurting people hurt people. It is a natural reaction. Our little Jack Russell terrier was recently hit by a car and eventually died from the injury. She was a sweet dog that wouldn't have hurt anyone, but when the driver got out of the car to try to help her, our dog bit the lady. The kind woman understood that Heidi was only reacting to her pain. People can be the same way. When someone grows up in horrible circumstances, they may develop a toxic personality that lashes out at other people. We can be slow to become angry if we can try to place ourselves in the other person's shoes.

It also helps us to understand circumstances. Although being hateful, spiteful, or disrespectful is never acceptable, when we under-stand the circumstances that led a person to act ugly toward us, we can have greater patience toward them. If possible, it pays to take the time to analyze everything about an event, if possible. If we do not, we may find that a quick temper results in folly. I can think of a lot of reactions in my life that led to foolish behavior. Arguments, by in large, are simply expressions of folly. They don't really accomplish anything except to drive a wedge between two people.

> "The end of a matter is better than its beginning; patience of spirit is better than haughtiness of spirit."
>
> Ecclesiastes 7:8

I am grateful for fact that God gives us His Spirit, and one of the fruits of the Spirit is self-control (Galatians 5:22-23). Because of this restraint in our lives, we can take the time to gain a firm grasp on our circumstances and not lash out in such a way that we do harm to our relationships with people. If you lack self-control in this area, it points to a deeper spiritual problem. We cannot work hard to manufacture spiritual fruit, like self-control. It comes as a by-product of our personal relationship with Jesus Christ. Work on your relationship with Jesus, and you will see this beautiful spiritual fruit popping out of your life.

The Wonderful Benefit of Anger Management

If you type the words *anger management* into Google, you'll get thousands of websites pointing to advice, therapists, books, and movies on the subject of getting control of your emotions. When we learn the important truth that the best form of anger management is the Lordship of Christ, we will find wonderful benefits taking place in our lives. One very familiar proverb is found in Proverbs 15:1 "A gentle answer turns away wrath, but a harsh word stirs up anger." Verse eighteen of that same chapter carries a similar message: "A hot-tempered man stirs up strife, but the slow to anger calms a dispute."

Life is all about choices, and people who have learned the discipline of self-control will be able to make choices about their reactions to people and circumstances. I once heard someone say that an argument can be very much like a fire. We can choose to be like water or like gasoline.

A gentle reply to someone who is angry or emotional will often times diffuse a situation and open the door to a resolution of the problem. A harsh word only adds fuel to the growing fire. I suppose the choice is to be reactive or to be responsive. When we respond to someone out of the overflow of the Holy Spirit of God who lives in us, the outcome is bound to be positive. If we choose to react in anger ourselves, we can be sure that a small flame has just turned into a blazing inferno.

Think about the message of Proverbs 16:32 in light of this truth: "He who is slow to anger is better than the mighty, and he who rules his spirit, than he who captures a city." What does it mean to be better than the mighty? Who do you think of when you read the word *mighty*? This word would certainly apply to people of power and prominence. *Mighty* would point to people in certain positions of authority or maybe even to people who wield certain power because of their financial means. Regardless of people's titles, they would be considered *mighty* if they are people of influence.

> "A wise man scales the city of the mighty and brings down the stronghold in which they trust."
>
> Proverbs 21:22

God says that when you can control your anger, you are better than the mighty. Better? In what way? I don't think the word points to financial bottom lines or of positions of power. Instead, I think it references influence. When you live a life under control and model behavior that points people to Jesus Christ, your influence is doubled or tripled.

When you read the second part of this couplet, you realize that the proverb writer was also thinking of a warrior. When a person can rule his spirit, he is greater than a mighty warrior who can capture a city. I can't help but picture a Rambo type of a guy who can go into a place and take it single handedly. God says that when you control your anger, you are mightier than a warrior. You can accomplish much when you can control yourself.

The greatest benefit of controlling our anger is that it honors the Lord. Although Solomon was surely thinking of himself as the king in Proverbs 14:35, the message of the proverb certainly applies to God: "The king's favor is toward a servant who acts wisely, but his anger is toward him who acts shamefully."

FURTHER THOUGHT

- Have you ever thought of anger as not being bad or wrong? What are some examples in your life where you've seen righteous anger?

- Why is it prudent for a person to conceal anger? When is it proper for anger not to be concealed?

- Having understanding helps us to manage anger in our hearts. Make a list of qualities in people or circumstances you will seek to understand *before* reacting toward someone with anger.

- Read Galatians 5:22-23. Because self-control is a fruit of the Spirit, or a growing expression of the Holy Spirit's presence in our lives, what are some things you can do to nurture your relationship with Christ?

- How does a gentle answer turn away wrath? Have you ever stirred up anger with your words? Do you find that you normally offer gentle answers to people? If not, what will you need to do so that you may respond in this way in the future?

- How are people who are slow to anger better than the mighty? How does this quality help you to accomplish Christ's mission in the world?

CHAPTER SIXTEEN
Resentful No More - Envy

"Facebook envy!" I've felt it before, but I just discovered that someone coined the phrase several years ago. To be candid, I'm excited for you if you have the privilege of scuba diving in the Caribbean or backpacking through the Alps, but in my weaker moments, I find myself wishing I could go on that adventure. Is it envy if I don't really begrudge your experience but only wish I were there too? Unfortunately, yes—especially if I let my wishes consume me. Dictionary.com says that envy is "a feeling of discontent or covetousness with regard to another's advantages, success, possessions, etc." So, if I happen to see Facebook pictures of you snow skiing in the Rockies, I may have a brief moment of discontent with my February, Georgia, thirty-five-degree rain showers. But if I let your vacation excursion consume my thinking and affect my spirit, then I'm in serious trouble. Gina Bellafante reported about this envy phenomenon and wrote, "Studies confirmed instinct: certain kinds of social media engagement drain happiness rather than generate it."[23]

Before we want to get Mark Zuckerberg back in front of Congress for yet another Facebook foible, let's remind ourselves that envy started long before 2004. In the latter part of the 6th century, Pope Gregory the Great reduced a previous list of eight offenses into what we now know as the seven deadly sins. Of course, the list of sins didn't come from his creativity but rather from the Word of God. He saw the need to list envy as one of the destructive seven.

What's the big deal with envy? Who cares if I look at your new F-150 and wish it were mine? God does. God doesn't mince words in Proverbs 14:30, "A tranquil heart gives life to the flesh, but envy makes the bones rot" (ESV). This proverb takes me to the crossroads and offers me a choice: life or rot.

It's interesting that the NASV translators chose the word *passion* instead of *envy* in Proverbs 14:30. The Hebrew word literally means "color produced in the face by deep emotion."[24] The word can be translated as jealousy, envy, passion, or zeal. It also can refer to several consuming emotions such as sexual passion or destructive envy. Because God created sexual passion and other positive passionate expressions, this proverb has to be referring to a destructive expression, such as envy. The fact that envy is connected to passion speaks to the controlling aspect of the vice.

The Destructive Pull of Envy

If you saw a sign warning you to avoid a certain road because the bridge was out, would you continue going forward? Curiosity may lead you to go check it out the first time, but what if you drove a couple of miles and discovered the bridge had indeed collapsed. In addition to this discovery, you also saw that if you happened to drive another fifty feet, your car would plummet into a 500-foot ravine and be dashed upon the rocks below. Would you be prone to take that road the next time you happened to be in the area? Of course not!

God tells us that envy may be worse than a 500-foot drop into sure destruction. Proverbs 27:4 says, "Wrath is fierce, and anger is a flood, but who can stand before jealousy?" There's our word again: jealousy or envy—being red in the face with passionate desire for something that is not yours. Look at the comparison presented in this passage. We see wrath and anger compared with envy, but God is stating that wrath and anger are no match for

> "The cure for the sin of envy is to find our contentment in God."
>
> Jerry Bridges

the destructive nature of envy. Consider the power of envy or jealousy by looking at the description of the lesser struggles of wrath and anger.

When this proverb says that wrath is fierce, the writer chose a word that not only means fierce, but also cruel. How is wrath cruel? You can think of it from two perspectives. Wrath can lead an individual to be cruel toward others without regard, but I'm led to consider the cruel nature of wrath in what it does to the one who is angry. When the writer chose the word for wrath, he picked a term to describe an extreme expression of fury. If you find yourself consumed with this level of wrath, you may find that wrath is indeed cruel to you. Unchecked anger is destructive by nature, and the destruction begins in the heart of the one holding it.

Anger is described as a flood. Have you ever been in a flood? Flood waters are dangerous and even deadly. They can destroy anything in their path. Wrath and anger in an individual are a powerful, formidable foe, but these are no comparison to what envy can do to the heart of a person. If you allow jealousy or envy to consume your heart, you are sure to fall.

Envy Can Be Deadly

We have seen that envy is destructive, but have you ever considered that it is specifically deadly? We have all heard the said stories of someone being killed by an envious individual who simply wanted the shoes of his victim. Because envy can be deadly, why would we welcome it in our hearts? It could be akin to picking up a rattle snake by the tail.

Would you like to have a glass of battery acid with your dinner tomorrow evening? No way! You wouldn't last ten minutes after ingesting something as deadly as battery acid. If you choose envy or covetousness, you will discover that it will eat a hole in your heart, not your stomach. Proverbs 21:25-26 warns us against the covetous heart of the lazy:

> *The craving of the lazy person is fatal,*
> *For lazy hands refuse to labor.*

All day long the wicked covet,
  But the righteous give and do not hold back. (NRSV)

The first line of verse 25 might lead you to wonder how a lazy man's desire would kill him. The sluggard, as the NASV calls him, may desire sleep, food, or Facebook. The next verse, however, helps us to understand that this craving is actually envy or covetousness for the possessions of others. The whole passage also hints to the fact that the lazy person craves what other people have, but he is not willing to work to get it. He lies around all day longing for what belongs to someone else.

This passage is a strong statement to challenge us to a healthy work ethic, but it also offers us additional counsel. Look at the last phrase. Upon your first reading, you may find the last line to be an odd contrasting statement to wicked desires. One approach to this concluding statement is that God is offering us the remedy to greed or envy: generosity. Giving to bless others is one of the most successful ways to overcome an unhealthy desire for more possessions. This phrase also offers the unwritten fact that for the righteous to give, they must work in order to have something to give. The contrasting statement of this proverb is the wicked covet, but the righteous give.

> *One of the greatest cures for envy and selfishness is generosity. Give until you want to give more.*

We can find many examples in the Bible of the painful consequences of envy. In Genesis, we find the conflict between Cain and Abel. Although the story carries with it various themes, the consequence of envy is prominent. I'm sure you know the story of how Cain brought an offering from his garden while Abel brought an offering from his flocks. Genesis 4:4-5 tells part of the story, "And the Lord had regard for Abel and for his offering, but for Cain and for his offering, He had no regard. Out of envy, Cain became very angry and his countenance fell." Naming reasons for why God didn't accept the offering is only conjecture because the Bible doesn't specifically provide any. However, something was amiss with Cain's heart, motive, or actions. Do you suppose there may have been a little red-faced passion in his fallen expression?

God came to Cain and asked him why his countenance had fallen. Obviously, God knew the answer, but He wanted Cain to process his attitude. Recognition of sin is the first step to overcoming it. Look at God's wise counsel in Genesis 4:7, "If you do well, will not your countenance be lifted up? And if you do not do well, sin is crouching at the door; and its desire is for you, but you must master it."

God's message to Cain is clear: either you master envy, or envy will master you. Here's one thing I've learned about envy: it is never content to simmer. It either moves toward the direction of repentance or it moves in the direction of destruction. Unfortunately for Cain, his envy moved toward destruction. God told him to "do well," which meant repent for his envious spirit, but instead, Cain opted for murder.

The Company of the Envious

I once heard the saying, "If you go to bed with dogs, you'll wake up with fleas." If that's the case, why would anyone want to sleep with dogs? I can't imagine anyone liking fleas. So, maybe your dogs do not have fleas, but what if flea-sharing dogs were life's only option? God warns us with words that lead us to understand that hanging out with the envious is just like sleeping with flea-bitten dogs who long to share their irritating pests with us.

You may find the pathway of the envious is crowded with other travelers. These fellow sojourners, however, will pull you with them into the pit, so consider the words of Proverbs 24:1-2:

> *Do not be envious of evil men,*
> *Nor desire to be with them;*
> *For their minds devise violence,*
> *And their lips talk of trouble.*

Why would anyone be envious of evil people? The only answer I can come up with is that from the outside, some evil people appear to be prosperous. At first glance, their lives may appear to be glamorous or successful; however, God says we must not fall into the trap of wanting their lives or their possessions. The reality is that everything about them is consumed in violence. They are constantly talking about trouble and will pull us into destruction.

God warns us in Proverbs 23:17, "Do not let your heart envy sinners, but live in the fear of the Lord always." If we envy sinners, we are not living in awe of God. We cannot envy the unrighteous and worship and serve God at the same time. Trying to mix those two lifestyles would be like trying to mix oil and water. It just can't be done. It doesn't matter what specific sin someone may practice, we should not envy them. Instead, we should *always* live in respect and awe of the Lord our God.

Proverbs 24:19-20 offers a challenging summary of the call to forsake the envious:

> *Do not fret because of evildoers*
> *Or be envious of the wicked;*
> *For there will be no future for the evil man;*
> *The lamp of the wicked will be put out.*

God is clear in this passage that those who are evil have no future. This concept must apply to this life and the one that is to come. It doesn't necessarily mean that evil people will die prematurely, though they might. It points to the reality that life apart from God and His will is not really life. When a person chooses to pursue evil, it's like he is living in darkness. Not only can he not see where he is going, but he ceases to be a beacon to provide guidance for others as well.

Envy's Alternative

We understand that envy is not good and should be avoided at all cost, but what is the alternative? Many places in the Bible offer a different path, including passages like Hebrews 13:5, "Make sure that your character is free from the love of money, being content with what you have." Paul also offered this counsel to young Timothy: "But godliness with contentment is great gain" (1 Timothy 6:6). Proverbs offers similar guidance.

Consider the message of Proverbs 30:8: "Remove far from me falsehood and lying; give me neither poverty nor riches; feed me with the food that is needful for me" (ESV). Allow that verse to simmer for just a moment in your spirit. Obviously, dishonesty needs to go. Neither poverty nor wealth seem to have a high value. The writer is saying that he wants only those things that are needful. This proverb carries with it a statement of contentment and a desire for only those things that really matter in life. It is so easy for us to come to a place in our lives where we think we *need* certain things, such as the latest iPhone or an upgrade on our vehicle. In fact, what we really *need* is contentment. Paul's words to Timothy in 1 Timothy 6:6 offer a great equation for joy: godliness + contentment = great gain. Here's a contrasting equation for destruction: selfishness + envy = great sorrow.

> *God, You have made us for Yourself, and our hearts are restless until they find their rest in You.*
>
> Augustine

FURTHER THOUGHT

- Can you relate to Facebook envy? Do you think our society has developed an acceptable envy? While this envy may be acceptable to our culture, do you think it's acceptable to God?

- What correlations to you see between passion and envy? Imagine teaching someone from another country to speak English. How would you define or describe envy to them?

- Review Proverbs 27:4 and think about the contrast between wrath, anger, and jealousy (or envy). Is it possible to stand against wrath and anger? Why would the writer insinuate that we cannot stand against jealousy?

- Proverbs 21:25-26 tells us that the craving of a lazy person is fatal. What are the cravings of a lazy person? What does that have to do with envy? Have you ever found those similar cravings eating away at your spirit?

- How might a generous spirit counter our tendency toward envy?

- Do you think with have a problem in our society with a lack of contentment? Why? How does one find contentment?

- Compare the two equations above that lead to great gain or great sorrow. What steps will you take to make sure the outcome of your life is gain?

CHAPTER SEVENTEEN
God's Gift, Our Joy - Marriage

"If I had to do it all over again, I would have done it sooner!" Done what sooner? Get a homemade peach milkshake from Chick-fil-A? While the milkshake is certainly worth getting as soon as possible, my friend and former pastor, Ed Sisson, was talking about marriage when he uttered those words. How many people do you know who talk about marriage in glowing terms? According to a Pew Research study, marriage is still quite popular, though cohabitation is on the rise. It is concerning to see that many people are opting to shack up instead of legally tying the knot. We typically think that it's only young people who decide to live together without marriage, but it seems that Baby Boomers are throwing nuptials to the wind at alarming rates. One interesting nugget of information from this study is that four out of ten marriages involve remarriage by at least one of the partners. It is also interesting to see that while many Americans chose to walk away from their spouses, they did not walk away from marriage.[25]

Sandra and I will be celebrating our 35th wedding anniversary this year. I have learned first-hand the truth of Proverbs 18:22, "He who finds a wife finds a good thing and obtains favor from the Lord." If I had to do it all over again, I would have done it sooner!

Another interesting statistic for me is that only 20% of married people reach the 35th anniversary milestone.[26]

> "Let the wife make the husband glad to come home, and let him make her sorry to see him leave."
>
> Martin Luther

When we first became engaged, Sandra was only nineteen, and I was twenty-one. We married about three months later. We were so excited and happy, but when we shared the news with other people, most did not share our glee. As a matter of fact, I didn't have one single person (other than our parents) who spoke positively about marriage. Most people made some type of sarcastic wise crack about the doom we were about to encounter. While these naysayers acted as if they were joking, I decided that they were revealing more about the state of their marriages than they intended to reveal. Where are the happily married people today? I hope you are one or that you aspire to be one.

I have some good news for all of us, regardless of the state of our marriages. God offers us sound guidance on how to have the marriage of our dreams. The Word of God is a great book on marriage, among many other topics, and we will find that Proverbs has much to say about how to fight for marital bliss.

Home Under Construction

As we are all works in progress, we can say the same thing about our marriages. Just because a couple scores a ten in their marriage today doesn't mean that tomorrow their marriage will be getting a gold medal. Have you personally experienced the ebb and flow of a fulfilling marriage relationship? I suppose good marriages are hard to find because they take a lot of work, and many people are simply not willing to make the investment.

Have you ever considered marriage to be a construction site? If you are married, do you feel that you should put on a hard hat upon entering your house? The message of Proverbs 24:3-4 offers a wonderful picture of the building project of marriage and family:

> By *wisdom a house is built,*
>   *and by understanding it is established;*
> *And by knowledge the rooms are filled*
>   *with all precious and pleasant riches.*

I'm sure it is obvious that this verse is not describing a real construction site. The focus of this scripture is upon building a home and not just a house. It is offering some key materials needed in order to build a wonderful marriage and a happy family. Proverbs 14:1 also uses the same imagery of building with a specific challenge to women, "The wise woman builds her house but the foolish tears it down with her own hands." Why wouldn't someone want to build her family and marriage? Only a fool destroys a family.

Look back at Proverbs 24:3 to uncover the first item on the materials list for a happy home: wisdom. We need wisdom in all circumstances, but we especially need it in our marriages. Good relationships are difficult to find and maintain, so we need wisdom if a happy marriage is going to be in our futures.

Do you remember my definition of wisdom I offered way back in chapter two? Wisdom is skill or expertise in living. As it applies to our current topic, wisdom would mean be a skillful or expert spouse. Wouldn't you love to be an expert? Actually, being an expert offers great dividends. I heard a few days ago that Matt Ryan, the quarter-back for the Atlanta Falcons, just signed a new five-year contract worth $150 million. He will receive $30 million per year to throw a football, hand it off, or even fumble it. That salary is mind blowing. How in the world did that happen? It happened to Matt Ryan because he is an expert. Your paycheck for being an expert husband or wife may not be quite $30 million per year, but you will still find the benefit for honing your marriage skills quite lucrative.

> "Christian marriage is marked by discipline and self-denial. Christianity does not therefore depreciate marriage, it sanctifies it."
>
> Dietrich Bonhoeffer

I hope the message of this first phrase is sinking into your willing heart. Just like Matt Ryan must work hard every day to be the top paid NFL quarterback, you must work even harder to be a top functioning spouse. Skill and expertise do not just fall into our laps while we are sucking down that peach milkshake. It takes a serious investment of time and labor in order to learn how to be a godly and effective spouse. My message to young couples during premarital counseling is if you are not willing to invest in the marriage, don't get married. For those of us who are married, if we're are not investing daily in developing marriage skills, start now!

When the scripture says your house will be built, it's obviously pointing to a strong marriage that not only stands the test of time, but also brings years of joy and fulfillment (better than a $30 million paycheck). I remember going to Guatemala to help with a construction project once and was impressed with the lengths to which these Guatemalan builders went to make sure the structure was strong. I learned that even though we were far from the coast, the building standard was to make sure a house could withstand a fierce hurricane. I think we should apply the same principle to our marriages. We never know when a strong storm will blow in, so we had better be adding the relational rebar every day. You will be strengthening your marriage as you grow in wisdom.

Great marriages and families are also established through understanding. This principle is key to a happy home and a strong marriage. The number one thing your spouse needs is understanding. You may think that the number one thing your spouse needs is fixing. It could be that your husband or wife needs a little tune up or maybe a major overhaul, but the first item you had better put into

> "A good marriage isn't something you find; it's something you make."
>
> Gary Thomas

your marriage shopping bag is understanding. Commit yourself to understanding his or her feelings, actions, thinking, and opinions. Many arguments are solved simply through understanding one another's points of view.

Because this passage can be applied to families as well as marriages, your children need understanding! I'll write more about parenting in another chapter, but we should all take time to listen to our children and understand how they feel and what they're going through. When we understand one another, we can stand one another, and we can stand with one another.

Do you see the third item mentioned in this wonderful palace your constructing called marriage? Knowledge! I know that each of these three words are used synonymously: wisdom, understanding, and knowledge. At the same time, they all build upon the previous word to show us a more complete picture of what is necessary for fulfilling relationships.

What do you think God meant when He led the writer to say *knowledge*? I have already alluded to the fact that if we're going to be happily married, we need a PhD that comes from studying our spouses. I think we probably also need a specialty degree in communication, conflict resolution, financial planning, goal setting, and spiritual development. There's at least one more topic that had better make our list of classes we shouldn't skip if we're going to have a strong marriage: theology.

A Love Triangle

The Bible is clear that God is love. The closer we walk with God the more we become like Him. I'm not saying that we become gods, but I am saying that God helps us to develop His character and attributes. God said in Romans 8:29 that He planned ahead of time, before the world was even formed is my guess, that His children would be conformed to the image of His Son. Wouldn't you love it if your spouse had the character of Jesus?

Christianity is a love relationship with Jesus that we experience not only personally but also collectively. If you are married, imagine your marriage being a little small group of three people who love each other deeply. The members of your group are you, your spouse, and God. I have often referred to this concept as a love triangle, but this triangle is guaranteed to help your marriage soar. Look at the equilateral triangle I have included below this paragraph.

> "When I have learned to love God better than my earthly dearest, I shall love my earthly dearest better than I do now."
>
> C. S. Lewis

Write your name on the line provided at the bottom left corner and your spouse's name at the bottom right corner. At the top, write the word *God*. Now, along the two sides of the triangle, draw arrows pointing from your names to God. The closer you grow to know God and to love God, the closer you grow to one another.

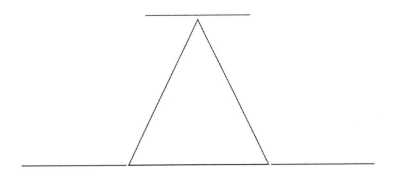

The Second Most Important Ingredient

I'll state it unequivocally: God is the most important factor, ingredient, or relationship necessary for a strong marriage. This fact means that the best thing you can do to have a strong marriage is to have a growing relationship with Jesus Christ. Second to God, however, is communication. I make that statement confidently be-cause many things about a strong marriage are built upon the foundation of healthy communication. Proverbs offers a lot of guidance on the topic of communication that applies to any relationship but especially to marriage.

I wrote previously about Proverbs 15:1, "A gentle answer turns away wrath, but a harsh word stirs up anger." Good communication never happens when conversation or conflict is driven by emotions. Conflict works to divide couples making them feel as if they are opponents. In order for couples to overcome conflict, they must set emotions aside, move the conflict out from between them, and join hands as teammates to conquer their new opponent: conflict. These steps will never take place unless good communication happens where gentle answers are offered in place of harsh words.

Proverbs 17:14 offers helpful counsel on overcoming a quarrel. Don't start one in the first place: "The beginning of strife is like letting out water, so abandon the quarrel before it breaks out." Picture a large dam with millions or billions of gallons of water behind it. A small leak forms in the dam, and if left to its own devices, that leak eventually becomes a major break. This proverb says that when conflict begins between two people, let's put it in the context of a married couple, it is like that small spurt of water from an opening in the dam. If the couple doesn't resolve the conflict quickly, a small spray will turn into a major breach. From the standpoint of a relationship, it's important to point out that this proverb tells us to abandon the quarrel and not the issue. Quarrels do not solve problems; good communication does. Quarrels are filled with emotional outbursts, and unfettered emotions lead to bigger problems.

The Bible teaches men to be the spiritual leaders of their homes, but providing spiritual leadership involves much more than just taking our families to church on Sundays. It also involves resolving issues in a godly way.

When you apply Proverbs 20:3 to a marriage relationship, it places the responsibility of spiritual leadership in the midst of conflict squarely into the hands of the husband: "Keeping away from strife is an honor for a man, but any fool will quarrel." It's possible this proverb uses *man* in a neuter sense that refers to all of humanity, but it could also be a direct challenge to men. It gives men a mandate. This truth means that in our marriages, we are to protect our marriages from unresolved conflict and always work to move our relationships toward peace and harmony. To do otherwise is to act the part of a fool.

Marriage is like anything that is worth having. It takes a lot of work, but in the end, the dividends are well worth the investment. While good marriages grow scarcer every day, God is honored and reflected in a marriage that is pure and peaceable.

FURTHER THOUGHT

- If you are married, can you remember hearing many positive statements about marriage from your friends or family members before your wedding day?
- List three benefits for your marriage of growing in wisdom.
- When considering the application of these verses to marriage, what is the difference between wisdom and understanding?

- Does your spouse need a little tune up or a major repair? Do you need a little work yourself? Regardless of your needs, or your spouse's, how does applying understanding strengthen your marriage?

- Spend some time looking at your "love triangle." What do you personally need to do in order to grow your relationship with Jesus?

- The last couple of verses mentioned overcoming quarrels. Do you have any conflict that may be keeping you from your greatest potential in your relationships? What can you do to move conflict out from between you and your spouse and become teammates?

- In response to the message of this chapter, what are some practical steps you can take to strengthen your marriage?

CHAPTER EIGHTEEN
Out of Bounds – Sexual Immorality

While nine out of ten people in America still say that adultery is wrong, other areas of sexual expression that were once considered immoral have gained wider acceptance in our country. For example, almost seven out of ten people say that sex between two unmarried adults is perfectly fine.[27] What's interesting, however, is that another study shows that 81% of Americans are concerned about the declining morality in our country.[28] When looking at the two studies, I wonder how most Americans would define *immorality*.

I suppose I'm not surprised, and I wonder how long it will take before more people see adultery as acceptable in our sex-crazed culture. Are you surprised? We are being inundated with sexual messages from television, the Internet, and just about every medium that may come to mind. Two out of three shows on television include sexual content. Sexual intercourse is depicted or strongly implied in one out of every ten television shows.[29] Is it any wonder that our nation as a whole is having a hard time deciding what is immoral in the 21st Century?

Although people may have difficulty discerning what crosses the line into immorality, God has no trouble making that distinction. Just because a human being wants to change a definition to make some act acceptable, God's definitions never change. The Bible has much to say about sexuality, and the bottom line is that sex within the boundaries of marriage between a man and a woman is good. God obviously thought it was a good thing because just after creating Adam and Eve, He told them to "be fruitful and multiply" (Genesis 1:26-28). God's plan, however, is that sex should remain within the context of a marriage commitment (Hebrews 13:4). It is when a society strays outside of those boundaries that people begin sliding down a slippery slope that leads to trouble.

Proverbs deals with a variety of topics, but you will see that the issue of sex or immorality is a common theme in the book. Remember that Solomon initially wrote his proverbs with a young man in mind, possibly his son. Sexual temptation in a young man's life is a strong contender for righteousness, so we shouldn't be surprised that Solomon chose to mention sexual immorality frequently.

Be Careful—Temptation Ahead

"Slippery When Wet." "Watch for Falling Rocks." We are accustomed to seeing warning signs every day. Throughout Scripture, we see exhortations as well, like "be careful," or "watch out." Proverbs 4:23 challenges us to be proactive when it comes to immorality, "Watch over your heart with all diligence, for from it flow the springs of life." This command is not just a statement telling us to dodge a surprising event, like the possibility of being stuck in the eye by a low-hanging tree branch. I think there is certainly a place for being on the alert so as not to be blind-sided by sexual temptations, but this verse is taking a little different angle. This passage says, "Watch over your heart." It carries an idea of protecting something that is vulnerable. I connect it to watching over a newborn baby or protecting an heirloom that has great value to your family.

When this proverb says to watch our hearts, we know it is not telling us to do more cardiovascular training. *Heart* is referring to the inner person, the control center of our lives. The translators could have just as easily used *mind*. Think of the air traffic control center for a major airport. My father-in-law retired as an air traffic controller after working that job for a little over 43 years. He worked in front of a radar monitor and directed the air traffic coming through the southeastern United States. Pilots had to follow his directions in order to get to their destinations safely. We also have a control center within our lives that ultimately determines our destination. I don't mean destination as in Atlanta or Chicago. Our hearts provide us guidance as to what kind of person we will ultimately become and whether or not we will honor the Lord with our daily decisions. It is within the control center of our

> "The heart is everything. It's the source of all life...the gateway to our emotions and our relationships. It's where we feel deep joy. It's where we experience deep pain."
>
> Gary Rosberg

lives that character is developed, and destinies are determined.

We are to watch over our hearts with diligence because the control center of our lives is under constant attack. The Scripture is very clear that we have a spiritual enemy who wants to wreck our lives, steal our joy, and taint our testimonies. If we do not diligently set up a watch over our minds and inner selves, we can easily fall prey to the wiles of the devil.

The NASV says we are to guard our hearts with *diligence*. The Hebrew word translated *diligence* is actually the first word of this verse in the original language. It is a term expressing totality. We might use the phrase *all in* to describe ourselves as being completely committed to something. God is saying that we are to give everything we have to guard our hearts because our hearts or minds are the main spiritual battlefield. In addition to the fact that our hearts are on the front lines of spiritual conflict, Jeremiah 17:9 says that our hearts are deceitful and difficult to know. We had better be 100% committed to guarding our hearts or we could be either seriously wounded or greatly deceived in this spiritual battle.

How do you watch over your heart or your mind with this kind of intensity? If you think about it, our inner selves are influenced by our senses. If we guard our hearts, we are being careful as to what we allow our senses to experience. We must be selective at what we allow our eyes to see and our ears to hear. This strategy is so important because springs of life flow from our inner being. Your control center will make decisions based upon the data you allow to enter, so be careful.

In the area of sexual temptation, we are so susceptible to evil influences through our senses. We must purpose to guard our minds, for if we do not, we will miss out on God's best for our lives. You will see that God warns us throughout Proverbs about falling into the trap of sexual immorality. Solomon doesn't mince words when he says, "Now then, my sons, listen to me and do not depart from the words of my mouth" (Proverbs 5:7). He is saying, "Do not mess up here, boys. This will destroy your life."

Solomon warns us about the adulteress and the negative consequences that will befall someone caught in the trap of immorality. Obviously, an adulteress would be a woman trying to woo a man into an immoral relationship, but I think we can personify all immorality with the term *adulteress*. Whether you are a man or a woman, we can all fall into the trap of sin's crafty enticements. Consider the plain warning of Proverbs 5:3-4:

> "God does not forbid sexual immorality because he wants you to be miserable [but because it] leads to brokenness, sad-ness, emptiness, death, and hell."
>
> Heath Lambert

For the lips of an adulteress drip honey
and smoother than oil is her speech;
But in the end, she is bitter as wormwood;
Sharp as a two-edge sword.

The Consequence of Immorality

"This can't be good." Have you ever mumbled that under your breath while looking at some mistake you made? Whether it's making a mistake on your tax returns or inadvertently charging something to the wrong account at work, you know that the fallout is going to be painful. As Solomon writes to warn his son or sons about the destruction of immorality, he also warns that there is no possible way that falling into the trap of sexual sin can turn out well.

In reading Proverbs, it seems sexual immorality in Solomon's day was represented mostly by adultery. While we would quickly place Solomon's marriage to 700 women, not to mention 300 concubines, in a category of immorality, that practice was not normal in Israel (1 Kings 11:3). Solomon evidently justified it in his mind, but he blatantly disregarded the law of God in taking foreign wives. His actions also seem to point to other moral failures in his life.

Regardless of Solomon's personal issues, sexual immorality has certainly expanded today from where it was 3000 years ago. They didn't have the temptations of pornography on the Internet or even the prevalence of premarital sex. I'm sure every now and then a young couple had sex before marriage, but the ancient Jewish culture made that kind of relationship difficult. When Proverbs deals with sexual immorality, adultery is typically the key concern, but I think we have to bring it into 21st Century terms and apply the warning to all of sexual sin.

Proverbs 6:32 underscores the painful consequences of continuing in a lifestyle of sexual immorality, "The one who commits adultery with a woman is lacking sense; he who would destroy himself does it." God designed sex and offers it to married couples as a wonderful gift, but when someone chooses to step outside of marriage for sexual fulfillment, that person is on a path toward destruction. This proverb says that anyone practicing adultery lacks sense. Why would God say that we lack sense if we choose adultery? The New Testament adds a little more clarity to the picture in 1 Corinthians 6:18, "Flee immorality. Every other sin that a man commits is outside the body, but the immoral man sins against his own body." Sexual immorality always exacts a painful price, so it doesn't make sense to pursue it. Only a fool would want to hurt himself. In the proverb above, God says that adultery leads to self-destruction. When it comes to sexual temptation, God says RUN!

> "Discretion will guard you, understanding will watch over you, to deliver you from the way of evil, from the man who speaks perverse things; from those who leave the paths of uprightness to walk in the ways of darkness."
>
> Proverbs 2:11-13

I think of an experience I probably had with all six of my children. I'm sure that somewhere along the way, I warned them all not to touch the hot stove or to stay away from the flames in the fireplace. "Hot," I would warn. "Do not touch." God equates the painful consequences of sexual sin to being burned by fire.

> *Can a man take fire in his bosom*
>   *And his clothes not be burned?*
> *Or can a man walk on hot coals*
>   *And his feet not be scorched?*
> *So is the one who goes in to his neighbor's wife;*
>   *Whoever touches her will not go unpunished.*
> —Proverbs 6:27-29

It is impossible to play with immorality and not get burned! How are we burned? It might come in the form of broken relationships, divorce, financial loss, or public humiliation. Sexual sin not only brings painful consequences to our lives, but also to the lives of the people we love. Have you ever considered the message of passages that speak of the father's sins being passed on to the next generations (Exodus 34:6-7)? Sexual sin is one of those sins that continues to affect our children and grandchildren. When marriages break up because of sexual sin, children suffer greatly. No one wins in divorce, but children are the ones facing the greatest loss. It is important for us to count the cost of sexual immorality and realize that not only will we be burned, but our children could also bear the scars for the rest of their lives.

God's Alternative

Even though sexual temptation is as normal as rain in spring, we should still run from its reaching tentacles. God's plan for sex from the beginning was to give it as a wonderful gift for married people. He said in 1 Corinthians 7:9 that it is better to marry than to burn with unfettered passion. I quoted Proverbs 18:22 in the previous chapter. It is true that "He who finds a wife, finds a good thing." Marriage is God's perfect alternative. Consider the message of Proverbs 5:18-19:

> *Let your fountain be blessed*
> *And rejoice in the wife of your youth.*
> *As a loving hind and a graceful doe,*
> *Let her breasts satisfy you at all times;*
> *Be exhilarated always with her love.*

God's alternative is always better than Satan's perversion. Based upon the consequences of sexual sin, God asks the question, "Why should you be exhilarated with an adulteress?" (Proverbs 5:20). Why would we be satisfied to pursue immorality when we can find lasting joy through a meaningful marriage relationship? Proverbs 5:23 concludes with strong words about the immoral, "In the greatness of his folly, he will go astray," but in the marriage relationship we can be "exhilarated always with her love" (Proverbs 5:19).

Grace Upon Grace

Most of us look at our past and feel some type of regret when it comes to sexual sin. For those who have been untainted by the pull of the world, I praise God for you. For those who have fallen into the trap of sexual sin, I have a word for you: grace. I am so grateful that God is the God of the second chance (and even third and fourth). God is not in the business of beating you up but rather lifting you up.

I love Psalm 40:2, "He brought me up out of the pit of destruction, out of the miry clay, and He set my feet upon a rock." As you look back at previous years, are you still trying to wash off the muddy stains? Maybe you're not in the pit anymore, but you still are feeling the pain of the burns from years past. Even though we may suffer with consequences of our failure, God is still in the forgiving business. Though we may bear the scars of our sin for the rest of our lives, God is like a healing balm to us.

My wife recently had two major surgeries that left prominent scars. It has been amazing, however, to see what time and a little vitamin e oil can do. God is for us better than healing oil, and He offer us the salve of grace and the benefit of peace. Forgiveness is an amazing blessing. Psalm 103:12 says that when we confess our sins to God, He spreads them from us as far as the east is from the west. Have you ever tried measuring the distance between east and west? It can't be done. God's grace is unmeasured, and His forgiveness is complete.

If you find yourself still in the pit today, remember that the Psalmist said that God brought him up out of the pit. God will bring you out of the pit, too, if you'll let Him. He is just waiting on you to call. He is standing beside your pit today with His loving arms outstretched toward you. Will you reach up and take His hand?

FURTHER THOUGHT

- How do you define sexual immorality? Do you think your definition agrees with God's definition in His Word?

- What are you doing to watch over your heart? Are you allowing your senses to bring ideas into your mind that could ultimately bring destruction? What can you do to insure the influences allowed into your mind will lead to actions that honor the Lord?

- Have you ever experienced the negative consequences of sexual immorality? It could be simply regret, or it could be something far worse. How has the consequence of sexual sin been like a two-edge sword in your life?

- How can you avoid being burned by the fire of sexual sin? Make a list of steps you will take so that sexual immorality will not be a part of your future. Consider issues such as the people with whom you spend your time, the websites you visit, or the programs you watch on television.

- Are you married? If so, how can you rejoice in your spouse and be exhilarated in his or her love?

- Do you have failure in your past from sexual immorality? Do you still struggle with shame or regret? What will you do today to receive God's grace?

- Are you in the pit of destruction now from sexual sin? Will you to reach up and let God pull you out?

CHAPTER NINETEEN
Building a Strong Foundation – Parenting

I remember offering parenting advice once to someone, but it didn't go over very well. I suppose that while my counsel may have hit unreceptive ears for a variety of reasons, two main issues come to mind. First, my friend didn't ask for advice, and second, I didn't have any children. This last reason reminds me of what American journalist, P. J. O'Rourke once said, "Every-body knows how to raise children except for the people who have them."[30]

I had an opinion, and I felt inclined to share it. Whether my opinion was correct is questionable. Now, six children later, would I give the same advice? I don't know, but I do know where I can find sound counsel that is always spot on. God's Word speaks truth on every subject imaginable, including parenting.

In my study of Proverbs, I discovered that God offers us more passages in Proverbs on parenting than a lot of other topics, and some of the general advice that applies to several different areas of life also applies to parenting as well. Why do you suppose He addressed this topic so thoroughly? I have no doubt it is because we need help. Parenting is not an easy task. How many parents of toddlers have about pulled their own hair out? Then, just when you think it's safe to write a book on parenting, your child hits puberty. You discover that you don't know anything after all. Mark Twain once suggested that when your child turns thirteen, put him in a barrel and feed him through a knot hole. When he turns sixteen, plug up the hole. Thankfully, God's advice is a lot more practical and will lead to great parenting success.

Proverbs 10:1 states, "A wise son makes a father glad, but a foolish son is a grief to his mother." First of all, this passage is not saying that a foolish son is not a grief to his father and that a wise son doesn't make his mother glad. If you are a parent, you probably know the proud papa (or mama) syndrome. Little Johnny does something note-worthy, and you can't quit talking about it. The contrast of this verse is not *father* and *mother* but rather *wise* versus *foolish*. Proverbs 17:25 carries a similar message, "A foolish son is grief to his father and bitterness to her who bore him." Because wise children make parents glad, and fool-ish children bring grief and bitterness to their parents, what must we do to help our children become wise?

Parenting is not for the Faint of Heart

"Anything that is worth doing, is worth doing well." I heard my mother say that a hundred times. I believe it is also in the book of what parents should say to their children. The axiom is true, however, and it's something that is not practiced very often in our instant society. Everywhere we turn, we discover shoddy work.

For example, I bought a house a while back and discovered that one of the electric outlets didn't work. When I pulled the outlet out of the wall, I discovered that it didn't work because the electrician had failed to attach a wire. The more disconcerting thing was that he left a bare, hot wire in the wall about four feet from the outlet. I had to tear out the sheetrock to find the dangerous wire and make the repair.

Here's another thing that my mother used to say, "Just because everyone else is doing it doesn't mean you should." Just because a lot of other parents are doing a poor job at the task of raising responsible, godly children doesn't mean that you should join them. Parenting is tiring, and good parenting is extremely challenging, but it is totally worth it. Proverbs 22:6 says, "Train up a child in the way he should go, even when he is old he will not depart from it." Let's think for a few moments about this powerful truth.

> "Each day of our lives we make deposits into the memory banks of our children."
>
> Charles Swindoll

If we will really labor at the task of training our children, they will benefit from it and grow up to be a blessing to themselves, to you, and to others. A lot of people misunderstand the concept of child training. If you really want to reap the benefits of this truth, you need to distinguish the difference between training and enduring. Your job is not simply to survive the parenting years.

Sadly, I have had many heart-broken parents tell me through the years that even though their children were going through a period of great rebellion, they were confident their children would one day return to the Lord because of the message of Proverbs 22:6. "After all," they would say with great conviction, "we always took them to church when they were young." While taking your children to church may have gotten them attendance pins, it doesn't necessarily guarantee you responsible, godly young adults years later. Training up a child involves so much more than taking him to church.

The Hebrew word that is translated as *train* is an interesting word. It could be translated as dedicate and carries with it the idea of repetition and consistency. Just from the standpoint of dedicating our children, this word says that we have set our children aside for the Lord and commit ourselves to growing them up to know and fear the Lord. A godly foundation in the lives of our children is essential if they are going one day to be solid, fruit bearing adults who enjoy the blessings of God in their lives. This type of dedication is a seven-day-a-week type of commitment where we are nurturing and discipling our children to know and serve the Lord.

The Aramaic equivalent to *train* is used to describe rubbing soothing ointment on a child's gums who was teething. In ancient times, a mother would chew up dates, spit out the juice and mashed up fruit back into her hand, and rub the substance on a young child's sore gums. It was a picture of love and sacrifice, but it was also a picture of consistency.

The writer is specific that we must train up a child *in the way he should go.* I've seen families spend more time and money to train up a son to be a professional baseball player than to walk with the Lord. There is a small chance that our boys will play professional ball, but there is a 100% chance that he will one day stand before the Lord. There is a 100% chance that he will face trials, struggles, opportunities, and divine appointments. Nothing wrong with baseball, but we need to make sure we are training our children *in the way they should go.* How much time are you leading your children to spend in God's Word? Are you teaching them to serve graciously and to sacrifice willingly? Are you helping them learn to be good stewards and to be faithful worshipers?

> "A child who is allowed to be disrespectful to his parents will not have true respect for anyone."
>
> Billy Graham

This passage is not hinting to the possibility that your godly child will stray and come back. It is more properly stating that if we train our children in the way they should live, they will live out that godly life, even when they are old. People sometimes use that verse to give them hope of repentance in their child's latter years. It could happen, but that is not the real message of that scripture. There's an old German proverb that addresses this concept from an opposite perspective, "What little Johnnie does not learn, John learns never." Our children's future as adults is dependent upon their training as children.

Disciplined to Discipline

If you enjoy disciplining your child, you probably need to see a therapist. However, if you refuse to discipline your child, a visit with a good counselor might still be your best move. Proverbs 29:15 says, "The rod and reproof give wisdom, but a child who gets his own way brings shame to his mother." That might be a good verse to have printed on a card to carry with you to hand out at Walmart in the toy department. At times, parenting seems to be like a contest, and you and your child are on opposite teams. My wife and I learned a long time ago that in the midst of the parenting contest, we must always win. This verse says that if we let our children get their way, it will eventually bring us shame. One of the greatest words that communicates love is *no*. It is easier to give in and say *yes* to our children, but the long-term consequences are painful.

Although discipline begins with saying no, it cannot stop there. Discipline can take all forms, and God even includes admonitions in His Word to spank our children:

> *Do not hold back discipline from the child,*
>   *Although you strike him with the rod, he will not die.*
> *You shall strike him with the rod*
>   *And rescue his soul from Sheol.*
>   —Proverbs 23:13-14

Spankings are not popular in our culture, and sometimes in reaction to child abuse, we may steer clear of this type of corporal punishment. Should spankings be avoided? Child abuse in any form is wrong, but God's Word is clear that spankings, when administered properly and lovingly, can have a very positive affect on our children. Other forms of discipline can also have a positive impact. The previous proverb says that spankings will not kill our children. Actually, it may even rescue them from death. Some translations say the child will be rescued from hell, but the word is literally Sheol, the place where all the dead go. It is simply referring to being buried. If we discipline our children properly, we could even save their lives.

Proverbs 13:24 offers additional insight to disciplining our children: "He who withholds his rod hates his son, but he who loves him, disciplines him diligently." You will obviously have to decide if you are going to use spankings in your parenting, but the Bible indicates that it has its place in child training. I am grateful that my parents lovingly spanked me, and we used spankings of one method of discipline with our children.

Have you ever let your children get away with something they did wrong even when they should have been punished? We do not avoid discipline because we love our children; we avoid it because we love ourselves. We don't want to worry with the issue at the time, or we don't want to interfere with whatever it is that we were doing. Discipline avoidance is actually very selfish. Proverbs

13:24 says we should discipline our children diligently. The Hebrew word means to do something *early*. It means that when our children need discipline, we don't beat around the bush. We get right down to business and take care of matters before matters take care of us. Showing love to our children may indeed be tearful at times, but in the end, you will cry tears of joy.

The Joys of Parenting

Although parenting is hard work, it is also rewarding work. Look at the message of Proverbs 23:15-16:

My son, if your heart is wise,
*   My own heart also will be glad;*
And my inmost being will rejoice
*   When your lips speak what is right.*

I have experienced the truth of this last proverb many times. I have seen my children make very wise choices, and I felt my heart swell with gladness. For example, the other day, I read a family text thread that was really a conversation between my children. They were talking about advice I've always given them to begin investing for retirement early. It thrilled me to see that they were following my counsel. If my child is wise, my heart will be glad.

I'll also never forget a difficult time in my life years ago when I was quite burned out and disappointed with everything, including myself. I was considering throwing

in the towel and pursuing any career other than the pas-
torate. My boys had a Christian band, and I decided to go
to one of their concerts. They were singing at a venue in
downtown Atlanta that seemed more like a bar than a
Christian concert hall. My
boys turned words around
that I had spoken in order to
get me to agree to let them
sing at this place: "You've
always said that we have to
meet people where they are,
so we can share with them
the gospel." What could I
say? It wasn't really a bar, but
it certainly wasn't a church
building. All kinds of people
gathered for the concert that

> **"When we let our
> children fly as arrows,
> we understand that
> we have been chosen
> by God to be the bow
> in their lives and point
> them in the right
> direction as we lead
> them to Jesus."**
>
> Crystal McDowell

night who really did need to hear the message of my boys'
music. It turns out, however, that I probably needed to
hear it most. God used one of the songs that my oldest
son had written to speak deeply to my heart that night. I
think God orchestrated that concert just for me.

As I look back at that night and the things my sons
said from that dimly lit stage, my inmost being rejoices.
When I hear my children say the things that are right, the
things that my wife and I taught them through the years,
I feel like shouting and crying at the same time. Parenting
is hard work, but in the end, the blessings are immeasurable.

Look how the New Living Translation presents Proverbs 23:24: "The father of godly children has cause for joy. What a pleasure to have children who are wise." Although I am sure the Apostle John was referring to his spiritual children in 3 John 4, I can certainly apply this message to my family and my children, "I could have no greater joy than to hear that my children are following the truth." The hard times of parenting our children are well worth it when our children are following the truth.

FURTHER THOUGHT

- Are you a parent? If so, can you think of a time that your child acted wisely and brought joy to your heart?

- Read again Proverbs 22:6, "Train up a child in the way he should go, even when he is old he will not depart from it." Make a list of some specific ways a parent could obey this command. Be specific. If you are a parent, are you willing to implement the items on this list? If you are not a parent yet, are you willing to make a pledge to obey Proverbs 22:6?

- Are you disciplined to discipline? Do you practice discipline avoidance? Write out several consequences of failing to discipline your children.

- Have you chosen to use spankings in your child training? Why or why not?

- What did you think about my comment, "We do not avoid discipline because we love our children; we avoid it because we love ourselves." What will you do in the area of discipline to make sure that you are communicating love to your child or children?

- Make a list of some of the joys of parenting. If you have grown children, you may be experiencing these joys now. If you don't even have children, this list can offer you guidance in future years.

- Pray for your children and for your role as a parent. Ask God to guide you in one of the most difficult yet rewarding tasks known to humanity.

CHAPTER TWENTY
The Power of Words

"Sticks and stones may break my bones, but words will never hurt me." To my embarrassment, I have a vague memory of saying that in playground banter when I was a young kid. Maybe it made me feel tough or vindicated, but there's one main problem with the adage; it's a lie. The only thing true with that statement is the first half of it. It's the second phrase that's problematic. Words *do* hurt. Words are powerful tools that can build up or tear down. James 3:5 states that even though our tongues are small members of our bodies, they wield great power. James also compared our tongues to a small rudder, which determines the direction of a great ship.

One of my favorite stories is about a young teen in my youth group many years ago. I was the youth pastor, and I decided to take my students on a wilderness river adventure. Because we lived in a big city, many of them had never paddled a canoe, but I figured I could whip them into shape with a few short lessons. I reviewed the finer points of canoeing as we stood on the side of a rain swollen river in central Texas. I waited until last to bring up the rear, and the two girls who launched just ahead of me were having a tough time. One of them, Karen, was a cowgirl through and through, but probably the closest she had ever been to getting in a canoe would have been when she fell into a water trough. Her dream was to grow up and work on a ranch.

I watched the girls paddle out into the middle of the river and begin to go in circles—literally. I grinned as I watched them circle, thinking they would eventually figure it out. I was wrong.

"Hey," I shouted out to them. "You girls having trouble?"

Karen, who was in the back of the canoe, looked back toward shore. "I think what we need is an utter."

I don't think an utter would have done them much good, but a rudder would have been quite useful. Our tongues are like rudders. They can direct us through life with ease, or if used inappropriately, we may find ourselves going in circles hurting others through our own mishaps.

> "*The tongue of the righteous is as choice silver; the heart of the wicked is worth little.*"
>
> Proverbs 10:20

Proverbs 12:18 speaks to the power of words, "Reckless words pierce like a sword, but the tongue of the wise brings healing" (NIV). Have you ever had someone speak a reckless word to you, and it cut you deep to the heart? Have you ever spoken such a word to someone else and seen the fallout from your careless act? The power of the tongue is a common theme in Proverbs, and God challenges us to use our words to bring healing and not destruction.

The Good

Words carefully chosen and thoughtfully applied can bring about such good in the lives of people. Proverbs 25:11 is one of my favorite proverbs: "A word aptly spoken is like apples of gold in settings of silver." This verse has always captured my imagination, though I have had a difficult time picturing apples of gold in settings of silver. The writer is describing something that is lovely and quite valuable.

When is the last time you saw an apple made from solid gold? I'm trying to imagine the value of something like that. I did my best to calculate the value of an average size apple made from gold, and if my math is correct, that apple would be worth about $350,000. This picture the proverb writer is painting for us has more than one gold apple in it. It's possible that this illustration offers over a million dollars just in gold apples, and then you have to calculate the value of the silver setting.

This word picture not only has monetary value, but it also offers beauty to the eye. Gold and silver have always caught the attention of human beings, and we forge beautiful jewelry out of these precious metals. Seeing a man speaking words of encouragement to his son or words of appreciation to his wife is also a beautiful sight to behold.

I was speaking somewhere once about communication, and I quoted Proverbs 25:11. I jokingly said off the cuff that this verse speaks more clearly to women than to men because we have a hard time appreciating the beauty of such an object as described in this passage. I tried to think of a manly version of the verse, but nothing came to me at the moment. After the session, someone slipped me a suggestion: "A word aptly spoken is like slabs of beef on plates of pewter." Now, that's something I can visualize!

This vision of loveliness comes in response to *a word aptly spoken*. What do those words mean? A word aptly spoken is the right word at the right time. There's no debate that the wrong word at the wrong time is a recipe for disaster, but what if we say the right word at the wrong time? This mistake usually results in a minimum of hurt feelings or possibly missing an opportunity for a powerful impact.

> "Write criticisms in dust and complements in stone."

Sometimes, we say the wrong word at the right time. This mistake can result in great offense as a result of our insensitivity. When we manage to say the right thing at the right time, it's like a sunny morning after a night of storms.

How do you say the right words at the right time? Appropriate speech certainly requires discipline, sensitivity, and knowledge. We need knowledge to know what to say and sensitivity to know when to say it. We need discipline in order to maintain our control when the moment is not right. Proverbs 20:15 expresses the value of applying knowledge to our conversations: "There is gold, and an abundance of jewels, but the lips of knowledge are a more precious thing." Although apples of gold in settings of silver have significant value, this proverb says that *lips of knowledge* are even better. This proverb points to the person who knows and understands both circumstances and people. He is a person who has acquired wisdom and knows how to deal with a particular situation in just the right way. The words he speaks reflects this understanding, and the result of his conversation is better than financial wealth.

We can use our mouths to speak that which is good in a lot of different ways. Speaking truth, for example, is a good thing:

> *Listen, for I will speak noble things;*
> *And the opening of my lips will reveal right things.*
> *For my mouth will utter truth;*
> *And wickedness is an abomination to my lips.*
> —Proverbs 8:6-7

Speaking compliments to people is another good way to use our words. Mark Twain once said, "I can live for two months on a good compliment." When was the last time someone picked you up with something as simple as an honest compliment or a pleasant word about you or your actions? Proverbs 16:24 says, "Pleasant words are a honeycomb, sweet to the soul and healing to the bones." If a compliment is *healing to the bones*, is it any wonder that Mark Twain thought so highly of it?

The Bad

Most of the world around us seems to be designed for discouragement and criticism. Where do we go for encouragement? Where can we find a positive word that will help us face the next challenge in life? The first answer that comes to our minds should be our families, and the second should be the church. However, families are just as broken as the people who make them up, and churches are simply larger communities of broken people.

The fragility of our society expresses the brokenness of humanity. We live in a world of hurting people, and I have always heard that hurting people hurt people. One reason we can hurt people is because our focus often times is upon ourselves instead of on others. Others can see our self-preoccupation many times by our own arrogant spirit. Look at the message of Proverbs 27:1-2:

> *Do not boast about tomorrow,*
> *For you do not know what a day may bring forth.*
> *Let another praise you,*
> *And not your own mouth;*
> *A stranger,*
> *And not your own lips.*

This proverb contains an important truth: don't brag. Let other people speak about your finer points, but you should make someone else the focal point of conversation. We have all been around someone who displays the attitude of this statement, "Enough talking about me.

Let's talk about what you think of me." Typically, people's preoccupation with themselves reveals a low self-worth and a need to boost their ego.

Proverbs 18:13 presents another important life principle: *Think before you speak:* "He who gives an answer before he hears, it is folly and shame to him." Have you ever been with people who answered your questions before you fully asked them? Did they ever answer them wrongly because they anticipated the incorrect question? God says making this a practice is folly and shame. We have come to a place in our culture where we do not ponder any longer. We seem to live our life in fifth gear, and we don't take time to think deeply about anything. This pattern is reflected in our relationships. God says that we are to take our time before giving an answer and make sure we fully understand the question.

The Ugly

Although people should choose to use their words for good, often times they opt for just the opposite. Sometimes, *bad* is too mild of a term to describe some people's wicked expressions. James 3:5-6 warns us about our tongues, "See how great a forest is set aflame by such a small fire! And the tongue is a fire, the very world of iniquity." Proverbs 4:24 states, "Put away from you a deceitful mouth and put devious speech far from you." This proverb literally says we are to put away a *crooked mouth.* The New Living Translation uses the word *perverse.* It presents the idea of setting aside any language that distorts, exaggerates, or flat out lies. Any words that do not speak truth must be put away. These words should not be a part of our lives or our vocabulary.

Another ugly use of our words is one of the seven deadly sins: slander. Proverbs 10:18 says, "He who conceals hatred has lying lips, and he who spreads slander is a fool." Slander is simply defaming another person with our words. Talking negatively about other people is just about as normal as breathing, but it is just as destructive as strangling. Gossip and slander are twin sisters, but slander goes to a deeper level of ugly behavior. One author described it this way, "Gossip collects someone's secrets and passes them to others; slander makes up its own secrets and broadcasts them wherever they will do the most harm."[31]

> "A soothing tongue is a tree of life, but perversion in it crushes the spirit."
>
> Proverbs 15:4

God hates gossip and slander, and we must hate it too. It destroys relationships and rips apart the church. Satan uses it to keep believers from being on mission. Jesus told us in John 13:34-35 that people will know we are believers by the love we have for one another. He also said in His high priestly prayer recorded in John 17 that the world will know that He is the Messiah by the quality of our relationships. Slander is detrimental to our mission, so is it any wonder that Satan works hard to make us slander? Can you imagine a world where everyone only speaks kindly to and of one another? That must be heaven. We should purpose in our hearts to bring a little taste of heaven to earth through our relation-ships with other Christians.

Needless to say, a number of other expressions could easily fall into the *ugly* category. We should abhor the ugly and cling to what is good. We want our words to speak life to others and represent the life that we have within us through Jesus Christ. Proverbs 15:4 states, "A soothing tongue is a tree of life." Are your words soothing to others? Proverbs 18:21 could be considered the theme verse in Proverbs about our speech: "Death and life are in the power of the tongue, and those who love it will eat its fruit." Your tongue carries a lot of power. It's a tiny member in your body, but it is huge in its affect in your life and the lives of others. How will you use your words? Will they bring life?

FURTHER THOUGHT

- Have you ever been hurt by someone's words? Do you still carry the scars? Can you relate to the words of the proverb, "Reckless words pierce like a sword?"
- Think about a time when someone said to you an "aptly" word. If you're studying this book in a small group, share your experience of someone sharing with you the right word at the right time.

- How are the lips of knowledge more precious than gold? Can you think of some good things you could say to others that would make a significant investment in their lives?

- Think about the message of Proverbs 8:7: "My mouth will utter truth." How can you apply that commitment to your life? What truth will you utter?

- What's wrong with boasting? Why is it included in the "Bad" section?

- Have you ever been a victim of gossip or slander? Why do you think people fall so easily into the trap of talking about other people?

- Because death and life are in the power of the tongue, what will you do to choose life?

CHAPTER TWENTY-ONE
The Best Policy - Honesty

What do these all have in common: black rhino, hawksbill turtle, Malayan tiger, and honesty? Did your guess have anything to do with the endangered species list? Although honesty is not a species, it is definitely endangered. The animals in that list are not only on the endangered species list, but they are on the *Critically Endangered* list. I'm afraid honesty may qualify for that list as well. What has happened to honesty in our culture? Dishonesty has become so normal that we don't seem to notice it anymore.

I remember a few years ago when I became aware of the Washington Post beginning to give out the *Pinocchio Awards* to people in the media who told the biggest lies. Most of the honors seemed to go to politicians. It didn't matter if people were Democrats or Republicans, this shameful recognition was doled out consistently. I was first stunned by the acknowledgment, but then, I was dismayed. The fact that we recognize the biggest liars, and this recognition doesn't stop the practice reveals that we have a problem. It seems that politicians don't really value the truth anymore, and our society has accepted the fact that most of them bend the truth a bit. Honest Abe must be rolling over in his grave. Sadly, politicians are not the only ones struggling to tell the truth.

Patty Ann Malley addressed the disturbing issue, "What are the consequences of lying today? A scolding? A spanking? Hellfire? Not anymore."[32] Although it may seem that people no longer face consequences for dishonesty, God's Word reveals a different scenario. Proverbs 12:22 says, "Lying lips are an abomination to the Lord, but those who deal faithfully are His delight."

Does God get Nauseated?

To say that something is an *abomination* to the Lord is to say that an act is detestable to God. It is a strong statement pointing to something as disgusting or repugnant. We might say that something makes us *sick* to our stomachs. It is interesting to scan through the pages of Scripture to note what God says is an abomination. If we have never struggled with homosexuality, we may put that at the top of the list because it is mentioned several times. For starters, God doesn't have a top-of-the-list category. *Any* sexual sin is an abomination to God.

Sexual sin is not the only disgusting act to our Creator. God gives us a list of other sins that He considers abominable:

> *There are six things which the Lord hates,*
> *Yes, seven which are an abomination to Him.*
> *Haughty eyes, a lying tongue,*
> *And hands that shed innocent blood.*

A heart that devises wicked plans
   Feet that run rapidly to evil.
A false witness who utters lies,
   And one who spreads strife among brothers.
               —Proverbs 6:16-19

Notice that a lying tongue made it to number two on the list of abominable deeds. Isn't that interesting? Someone lies to us about a political matter, and we shake our heads and give him four Pinocchios. God, on the other hand, sees it as an abomination. We make light of something that God obviously deems as quite serious.

When you read through the early pages of the Old Testament and notice the things that God calls an abomination, you will quickly see the designation often deals with an act that relates to idolatry. Worshiping other gods is an abomination to the One true God. Maybe one reason that God detests dishonesty so much is because lying reflects the nature of God's archenemy.

Jesus spoke candidly about Satan in John 8:44:

"You are of your father the devil, and you want to do the desires of your father. He was a murderer from the beginning and does not stand in the truth because there is not truth in him. Whenever he speaks a lie, he speaks from his own nature, for he is a liar and the father of lies."

I wonder how many Pinocchios Satan would get. Our enemy does not stand in the truth because there's not an ounce of truth in him. Should we be surprised that when we act like Satan that God is disgusted? Lying could be viewed as a form of idolatry.

Before we begin to think that God grades sin on the curve, I need to say that all of sin is a stench in God's holy nostrils. He hates it all. Because of sin, Jesus had to die, so any sin is repugnant to our Heavenly Father. Even though all of sin is equally bad in God's eyes, however, He does specifically speak out against the sin of dishonesty.

Reflecting Our Father's Nature

It makes sense that we should be like our heavenly Father. Being like Him is God's desire for us, to be like Him. Proverbs 13:5 speaks to the fact that we will share God's opinion of dishonesty: "A righteous man hates falsehood, but a wicked man acts disgustingly and shamefully." Since lying reflects Satan, honesty reflects God. Someone who habitually lies gives the indication of having the devil as his father, but someone who hates falsehood expresses the righteousness of God. The second half of Proverbs 13:5 offers a contrast to the first half. What are the disgusting and shameful acts alluded to here? The first half of the couplet provides our answer: falsehood.

When this passage says that the wicked, who speak lies, act disgustingly, it is literally saying they stink. Lying is a vile stench in the nostrils of God, like a dead animal on the side of the road. Once again, I connect this concept to worship. Leviticus 1:9 refers to the burnt offerings that were given to God in worship as a pleasing aroma to the

Lord. When we lie, our act is the opposite of worship and sends up a repugnant smell to the Almighty.

Not only do lies disgust God, but they also cause a stink to all of those around us. Dishonesty destroys relationships and taints our testimonies. It robs us of credibility and hinders our effective ministries. It's no wonder that lying is considered shameful by the One whose opinion really matters.

Strengthening Community with Others

Community is important to God. He even exists as a community within Himself. Do you remember in Genesis 1:26 when God said, "Let us make man in our image?" Who was He talking about when he used the plural pronouns us and our? Although the word *trinity* is not used in the Bible, the concept is found throughout Scripture. In the very beginning, we see God's triune nature expressed in this early verse, and we discover that part of God's nature is expressed in community. Therefore, we reflect God's nature better in community with others than alone.

God hates anything that mars His image, and when dishonesty hurts our relationships with one another, God's image is not reflected so strongly in His church. Proverbs 16:28 says, "A perverse man spreads strife, and a slanderer separates intimate friends." Perversity is like a contagious disease, and the fallout always shows up in anger, bitterness, and conflict. Even close friends can be affected by slander. Have you ever been separated from a close friend because of dishonesty? Maybe the reason

God hates dishonesty so much is because He loves us even more. It hurts Him to see us hurt or to hurt someone else.

Think about the role of honesty at work. Politics is not the only place in our culture that is scarred by dishonesty. The workplace all across our country is negatively impacted by deceit. Columnist Zoe Henry stated that from employee theft and fraud alone, companies can lose as much as $50 billion. Theft at the workplace can be measured, but it is impossible to know the full, negative impact of other forms of dishonesty such as lying. A few years ago, Careerbuilder.com conducted a survey and discovered that 20 percent of people tell lies at work each week.[33] I'm surprised it was only 20 percent. I have a feeling some of them were lying.

> *"Truthful lips will be established forever, but a lying tongue is only for a moment."*
>
> Proverbs 12:19

Isn't integrity like a breath of fresh air. My family and I just had a yard sale this past weekend. I think I'd rather have root canal, but we did it anyway. I've never had a root canal, but I can't imagine it being worse than a yard sale. We had the yard sale because one of our sons is going to Europe to do mission work for a year, and we thought it would be a good way to help fund his trip. Because we didn't sell much on the first day, we just left the stuff out in the yard for day two. At one point, no one was even home, but all of our prized junk was still on display. When my wife returned home, she discovered that someone had stopped by to "shop" and had actually purchased something. The shoppers were long gone, but they left the money under a rock on a table.

Not only does integrity bless our friends and coworkers, but it also blesses our family. Proverbs 20:7 says, "A righteous man who walks in his integrity—how blessed are his sons after him." The word *blessed* points to extreme happiness or fulfilling joy. I mentioned earlier about the sins of the father being visited on the children, well, in this case, the righteousness of the father is visited upon the children. The offspring of the righteous man are blessed because of his integrity. Our choices and character have a huge impact on our families.

The Consequences of a Life of Honesty

Everything has a consequence. I know that many people live as if there are no consequences for their actions, but the fact is that there is always a payday. We are warned in Scripture that even our most secret sins will eventually be exposed (Numbers 32:23). Even as the ramifications of dishonesty are negative and painful, the consequences of integrity are a blessing. For example, according to Proverbs 11:3, integrity will provide direction in our lives: "The integrity of the upright will guide them, but the crookedness of the treacherous will destroy them."

Did you notice the contrast of that previous proverb? Guidance versus destruction. If we choose integrity, we find guidance. Who doesn't want guidance in life? The insinuation of this verse is that we have guidance or direction down the right path that leads to blessing. The contrast is that if we choose a life of dishonesty or *crookedness*, we will be destroyed. This means our relationships will be destroyed, our careers will be destroyed, and if we are not Christians and never repent, our souls will be destroyed.

Think about the application of Proverbs 16:13 to your life: "Righteous lips are the delight of kings, and he who speaks right is loved." Odds are we will not be entertained by true kings in our lives, but you could apply this principle in general ways to the people who are in authority over your life. These authorities could include your employer, for ex-ample. What if you replace the word *king* with the words *your employer*? Do you think that is a proper way to apply this biblical principle? I do. "Righteous lips are the delight of your employer, and he who speaks right is

> "*And my inmost being will rejoice when your lips speak what is right."*
>
> Proverbs 23:16

loved (by the boss)." Do you want to excel at work and be the next person selected for that promotion? Be honest.

How would you like to be secure in your life? Proverbs 10:9 states, "He who walks in integrity walks securely, but he who perverts his ways will be found out." What does it mean to walk *securely*? The Hebrew word translated *securely* means to walk with confidence and safety. It means living without care. The thought that crossed my mind was something I heard many years ago as a child. "If you always tell the truth, you never have to remember what you said." Telling the truth surely removes some of the stress or care from life. You certainly never have to worry about falling in the hole you dug for yourself.

In the long run, honesty always pays dividends. It blesses our relationships and strengthens our careers. Above all things, it honors the Lord. When we choose to be people of integrity, we live a life of worship and praise to our Righteous Lord. Why would anyone opt for destruction, sorrow, and danger when a good name is to be more desired than great wealth" (Proverbs 22:1)?

FURTHER THOUGHT

- List a few evidences that indicate our society no longer seems to value honesty.

- God could have just said that lying is sin. Why do you think He said lying is an *abomination*?

- Think about the difference between hating falsehood and acting disgustingly and shamefully. How might it be obvious in your life if you hate falsehood? What are some actions, opposite of hating falsehood, that are disgusting and shameful?

- How does speaking the truth strengthen community with other people?

- Have you ever seen co-workers who lacked integrity? Do you think theft in your workplace is common? What difference would it make where you work if all of the employees were honest?

- Make two lists. In one, write down the consequences of integrity, and in the other, create a list of the consequences of a life lacking integrity.

- Are you an honest person? Do you need to make any adjustments in your life so as to be a person of integrity?

Chapter Twenty-Two
Off to Work We Go

Self-made steel tycoon and philanthropist Andrew Carnegie once said, "Anything in life that is worth having is worth working for." My parents drilled that message into me from time I was a young boy. They taught me that if I wanted something, I had to work hard to get it. My mother told me a million times, "You can do anything you want to do if you want to do it badly enough." The bottom line is that there is no substitute for hard work.

I began preaching when I was fourteen-years-old and went on staff at a church when I was seventeen. I officially became a senior pastor at the ripe old age of nineteen. I am so thankful for patient people and church members who loved me no matter what I did or didn't do.

I remember one time taking some children home after a kids' event and striking up a conversation with a boy who had begun coming to Kids Club that summer. He was sitting in the passenger seat while I was driving the van load of kids to their homes. He asked me what I did. That was a legitimate question, and I wasn't real sure how to answer it.

"Well," I drew out as my brain turned the question over and over, "I'm the pastor of the church."

"Yeah, but what do you do?"

"Uh, well, I study, and I pray. I preach three times a week."

"I know, but what do you do?"

I figured that he was really getting into the whole idea of ministry. Who knew? Maybe God was calling him to be a pastor, too. "I lead activities for the children, like today. I meet with people and pray with them. Sometimes I visit sick people in the hospital, and sometimes…"

He interrupted me with a great deal of exasperation. "Don't you ever do any real work like my dad?"

What do you say to that? Now that I've been in ministry for many years, I have learned many important lessons. One of them is that no matter what field you pursue, if you want real success, you've got to be willing to roll up your sleeves and get down to work. I'm sure I've gotten callouses from being a pastor, like the time I had to dig a French drain around the back of the sanctuary to keep the storm water on the outside of the building. Most of the hard work of ministry, however, hasn't been the manual labor type of work, but it has still kept me up many a night.

> "Commit your works to the Lord and your plans will be established."
>
> Proverbs 16:3

I have heard people say that working came as a result of mankind's fall in the Garden of Eden. No, that's not true. Adam was actually told to work before he sinned. Work is not part of the curse but rather part of the blessing.

Working Out of Blessing

Riches can be measured by a lot of different types of currency. I have always felt like I was a rich man, even though I've never had a lot of money in my bank account. Proverbs has much to say about wealth, and some of the comments seem to speak specifically to financial gain. As you study through this section, I encourage you to allow your mind to expand on this topic so as to grasp the fact that your future riches may have nothing to do with your 401K or real estate investments. In other words, your bottom line is not always your bottom line.

Though we will consider wealth from a variety of perspectives, God clearly points out that financial gain comes to those who work hard for it.

Poor is he who works with a negligent hand,
But the hand of the diligent makes rich.
He who gathers in summer is a son who acts wisely,
But he who sleeps in harvest is a son who acts shamefully.
—Proverbs 10:4-5

This proverb reveals clearly part of the equation of poverty: a negligent hand. A negligent hand comes from a lazy person who is slack and derelict in his duties. He looks for the short cuts and the easy way out. He may work hard, but he works hard to get out of work. The parallel in the above proverb to a negligent hand is the son who sleeps in the harvest. He does not have a strong work ethic.

The contrasting son is the one who works diligently. There is typically financial gain for the person who is willing to work hard and work smart. I realize that "rich" may have varying definitions, but the general principle of this verse states that you will have financial gain, and a lot of it, if you are willing to work hard.

What does this truth mean for you? If you are always looking for the easy way out, I don't think you have a *diligent hand*. If you never volunteer for the tough jobs and always clock out on the hour, you are not a picture of a diligent worker. Clock punchers and lap counters rarely ever make it to the extra mile. While there's not much traffic on the second mile, you will also find that there is an abundance of opportunity. It's easier to shine when there's no one blocking your luster.

I tell young people that they should go into work early and leave late. They should give their bosses their cell phone numbers and tell him that if he ever needs someone to work extra, they will be glad to volunteer. Work with a song on your heart and a whistle on your lips. Wear a smile on your face and grace in your spirit. Be a servant to all without expectations of others. Don't just go the extra mile; go two or three more past that. Newt Gingrich said, "Perseverance is the hard work you do after you get tired of doing the hard work you already did."[34]

Working Through

I learned how to "work through" as a long-distance runner. I thought football taught me the lessons of perseverance, but training for my first marathon gave me a whole new appreciation for the old saying, "No pain, no gain." Proverbs 15:19 says, "The way of the lazy is as a hedge of thorns, but the path of the upright is a highway." This proverb presents life as if it is two different realities, but many times, both the lazy and the upright start in the same place. The difference is that while the lazy person sees thorns, the diligent person sees roses.

This proverb says that a lazy person is hindered by a hedge of thorns, but the upright person, or diligent person, refuses to be stopped by this obstacle. Life is full of hardships, and the person bound for success must work through those hardships. This truth means that sometimes we work through problems with people or financial challenges. We work through physical strain or

> "The desire of the sluggard puts him to death, for his hand refuses to work."
>
> Proverbs 21:25

through superiors who do not see situations in the same light as ourselves. We work through the incompetence of others and the dereliction of lazy people around us. We refuse to take no as an answer and defeat as an option. We will go down the highway to success, even if we have to make the highway ourselves. God refers to this approach as being the *path of the upright.*

I am grateful that God didn't stop at various obstacles along the way. Traveling to Bethlehem before His birth must have been a challenging way to begin his life on earth. If Jesus had been the typical person in today's society, He could have blamed failure on the fact that He was first laid in a manger or spent the first days of his life smelling animal dung. Jesus could have blamed poverty or endangerment. He could have shifted blame to the disciples he had chosen, or He could have disparaged the Roman soldiers. He could have blamed the Father for turning His back on Him. These obstacles presented challenges, but they didn't thwart His mission. Jesus worked through His challenges in order to complete His mission, and we must do the same thing.

Another obstacle we may face along the road to success is pleasure. Pleasure is certainly not a bad thing, but if we let it consume us, poverty will soon be our taskmaster. Proverbs 21:17 states, "He who loves pleasure will become a poor man; He who loves wine and oil will not become rich." If pleasure becomes your god, you will do anything and sacrifice everything in order to experience it. How much money have people blown in their search for pleasure? While pleasure is certainly enjoyable and preferred, it is not our objective and destination.

Proverbs 20:13 tells us of another major obstacle some people face: "Do not love sleep, or you will become poor; open your eyes, and you will be satisfied with food." Just as it is wrong to rob your body of needed sleep, too much sleep can rob you of opportunities. This proverb could be the ancient version of our "early bird gets the worm" saying. If you want to succeed in life, you must be willing to rise, and shine.

Working From

We work out of the blessings, through the challenges, and from a proper perspective. We can experience blessing only because God is willing to bless those who seek Him. The end product is never about money, power, or position. It is always about relationships. First, it's about our relationship with God, and secondly, it's about our relationship with humanity. We must always keep the proper perspective in mind. I used to have a little postcard with an acrostic from the word JOY. If you want real joy, you must put Jesus first, others second, and yourself last.

Proverbs 28:27 helps us with perspective: "He who gives to the poor will never want, but he who shuts his eyes will have many curses." God always calls us to be generous people. He is such a giving God. We are never more like Him than when we are giving to others. One problem with success is that it can cause us to become greedy. One of the greatest ways to overcome greed is with generosity. God says that if we have a heart to give and bless the poor that we will never have need ourselves. We must always work from the perspective that God wants us to bless others. If we shut our eyes to the needs of others, we will experience the consequences of living the tight-fisted lives of cold-hearted people.

The United States used to top the list of the most generous countries in the world. This rank is based upon how many people recently gave a financial gift to a charity. We lost the number one position a while back. Do you know who is the most generous country now? Myanmar. Do you even know where Myanmar is located? It is interesting that the people of Myanmar give to help others because they think they're improving their chances of the next life being better than this one. We should give in this life because we know that the next life is better than this one.

> "But godliness actually is a means of great gain when accompanied by contentment."
>
> I Timothy 6:6

We also need a proper perspective of satisfaction. A lot of surveys have been taken through the years asking people how much money they would need to be satisfied. The typical answer is just a little bit more. Proverbs 27:20 offers a strong warning: "Death and Destruction are never satisfied, and neither are the eyes of man." I'll venture to say that the eyes of man are never satisfied because they are looking at the wrong thing. Hebrews 12:2 says we should fix our eyes on Jesus. If we fix our eyes on anything else, we're going to eventually come up empty.

One final perspective should be in the front of our minds. We should work from financial freedom. Do you find yourself in financial bondage through debt? Proverbs 22:7 says, "the borrower is servant to the lender." When we are encumbered with the chains of debt, we will find our options are quite limited. In order to experience financial freedom, we have to make some very important decisions.

Pay cash and avoid credit. Credit cards are destroying our society. They offer a means by which you start at the bottom and then dig yourself a hole. I heard about a man whose wife's credit cards were stolen but he didn't call to cancel them. He said the reason he didn't cancel them was because the thieves were spending less than she was. I suppose that story is really not true, but the problems of credit card debt in our country are climbing by the minute. Compounding interest is also compounding problems.

Avoid unnecessary debt. Remember that when you borrow money from someone, you are a servant to the lender. The lender holds all of the strings. We must always ask if going into debt is necessary and is it wise. Is there a better way to move forward without getting into deep debt? Steady plodding as opposed to instant gratification is usually the best route to take. Proverbs 21:5 states, "The plans of the diligent lead surely to advantage, but everyone who is hasty comes surely to poverty."

Always be generous to give. Proverbs 22:9 offers the call to generosity: "He who is generous will be blessed for he gives some of his food to the poor."

The book of Proverbs challenges us to work hard and to work out of the wonderful blessings God has given us. Scripture also calls us to work through any obstacle in our way and work from a perspective of financial freedom. If we follow through with these commitments, we will experience the smile of God on our lives.

FURTHER THOUGHT

- How would you define working with a negligent hand (Proverbs 10:4)?

- Would you say that our society has become lazy? If so, what do you think has caused this problem?

- What does "working through" mean to you? Do you have any issues you have to work through?

- When you look at "the hedge" (see Proverbs 15:19), do you see thorns or roses? What will you need to do to make sure you always see the roses and the highway of blessing?

- How can you gain a proper perspective of work? Do you have real JOY (Jesus first, Others second, and Yourself last)?

- Are you a generous person? Do you give to people in need on a regular basis? Make a list of five things you can do this week to express generosity. Share your list with someone.

- Are you financially free? Make a plan that will lead you to being debt-free and able to be more generous.

CHAPTER TWENTY-THREE
The Path of the Arrogant

"If you even dream of beating me, you better wake up and apologize." These words came from the lips of one who claimed not to be the greatest boxer of all time but the double greatest: Muhammad Ali. After watching his career, it's hard not to agree with him, but his arrogance never sat well with me. I usually wrote it off as a show.

Since my early observations of boxing's heavyweight champion of the world, I've seen the arrogance of other professional athletes and marvel that they don't embarrass themselves with their banter. It is obvious that these professional athletes, who think so highly of themselves, have never read Proverbs 8:13, "The fear of the Lord is to hate evil; pride and arrogance and the evil way and the perverted mouth, I hate." We should sit up and take notice of something when God says He hates it. In this case, He hates pride and arrogance.

A Path to Disgust

What really turns your stomach? I don't mean like some type of food that you hate but rather something that is offensive deep in the depths of your soul. A couple of years ago, my son Jonathan and I joined a small team of missionaries to do research on unreached people groups in the Andes Mountains of Peru. We spent over a week backpacking through the mountains and meeting people in various small villages along the way.

One day, we came across a man lying in the bushes, and his little girl squatted beside him trying to wake him up. She couldn't have been much older than six or seven. It turned out that he was drunk. It was evidently not the first time the young girl took care of her inebriated father. I felt strong disgust deep inside of me. It was disgust for a father who would treat his family with such contempt and for the abuse of a substance that wrecks the lives of people all over the world.

What disgusts you? Proverbs 16:5 tells us that pride disgusts God: "Everyone who is proud in heart is an abomination to the Lord; assuredly, he will not be unpunished." Abomination. There's that word again. So, lying is an abomination to the Lord, and now we discover that pride is too.

> "When pride comes, then comes dishonor, but with the humble is wisdom."
>
> Proverbs 11:2

Why do you think God has such a reaction to the arrogance of humanity? British pastor and evangelist Alan Redpath offered an interesting answer, "Pride is the idolatrous worship of self, and that is the national religion of hell."[35] God sees pride as an abomination because it breaks the first commandment of having no other God before Him. In this case, the god of the arrogant is self.

Certainly, we all see the problem with worshiping self. We're not God. If we worship self, we are worshiping a

flawed deity, that is not a deity at all. Although God's
nature demands worship, He knows that we will never
experience abundant life and true joy unless we are in a
right relationship with Him. While God should be first
and foremost in our lives, from God's perspective, the
Ten Commandments are about us. By following God's
commandments, we enjoy life as it should be lived.

When Proverbs 16:5 ends with the words, "assuredly,
he will not be unpunished," they are referring to the consequences of following false gods. If you choose to
worship self instead of surrender to Christ, the consequence is eternal separation from God. If a Christian slips
into a life of pride, he, too, will face negative consequences. I do not believe Christians will lose their
salvation, but the consequence of living out of the will of
God is severe: missed opportunities, lack of purpose,
disappointment, and multiplied sorrows, to name a few.

A Path to Destruction

Destruction seems to be a familiar word in Proverbs. An
image comes to my mind of a bicycle path my brothers
and I enjoyed when we were children. When I lived in
Augusta, Georgia as a child, our house was not too far
from the Savannah River. Although I never risked going
so far as the river, I did play around near a canal leading
to the river and in some of the creeks feeding the canal.
One place offered a narrow path that seemed just a little
wider than bicycle wheels. The path ran down a hill,
through a gully, and back up the other side. On each side

of the path in the bottom of the gully was a swamp. We would start on one side and fly down the hill on our bikes, hoping to keep our wheels on the path.

My brother had killed fat water moccasins in those swamps, and we had seen all manner of creepy things around, so there was no telling what might happen if we ventured off the path. To start with, our mother didn't know we were living so dangerously. If she had known some of the crazy risks we were taking, we would have been in big trouble. If we had fallen into the stinking water, who knows what kind of swamp monster would have attacked us.

Destruction! I took risks as a child that I now know I never should have taken. I wonder if we take childish risks as adults. Playing with sin is a major risk that can be worse than the bite of a snake. Proverbs 16:18 says, "Pride goes before destruction, and a haughty spirit before stumbling." One reason God hates pride so much is that He loves us so much. He knows that pride leads to a slippery swamp filled with all manner of poisonous vermin. God doesn't

> "*True humility is not thinking less of ourselves but thinking of ourselves less.*"
>
> Rick Warren

want us, His loved ones, to fall prey to the enemy of our souls.

Pride is a major barrier to becoming a Christian. In order to be saved, we have to repent of our sins and surrender to Jesus Christ as our Lord. Pride and surrender cannot coexist. Is it any wonder that God led Solomon to say that pride goes before destruction? Without surrender to Christ, you are hell bound.

We can also experience other types of destruction. Pride is one of the biggest challenges to a healthy marriage and to balanced, successful parenting. With a little thought, you should be able to see a lot of destructive possibilities in your family if you choose arrogance over surrender or selfishness over service.

A person who has a haughty spirit is unable to see his faults. We all have faults. The fact is that we have more faults than we even see, faults that harm our relationships and hinder our potential in life. We must own our faults and seek forgiveness from others or we will surely stumble. This stumbling may be seen in broken marriages and rebellious children, but it can also be seen in lost jobs and missed opportunities. Maybe that's one reason Proverbs 29:23 says, "A man's pride will bring him low, but a humble spirit will obtain honor."

Living Within Bounds

I played football some in high school, and because I played quarterback, I periodically had opportunities to shine. I have to confess that my shine was more like a silver utensil that desperately needed to be polished, but even dull silver can catch a little gleam from the light. I remember one play where I faked a pitch out and kept the ball to run a quarterback option. Because I opted to keep the ball, I sprinted toward the open sideline. I don't remember how many yards I ran, but it was quite impressive. The thing that was not impressive was that I stepped out of bounds not too far from the line of scrimmage. See what I mean by dull silver?

God gives us boundaries for life, and choosing arrogance is like running out of bounds. To live within the boundaries and to experience the blessings of God, we must choose humility. Why not be humble? I sometimes hear kids criticize someone's pride by saying, "He thinks he's all that." The reality is that none of us are all of that. God is!

Proverbs 15:33 says, "The fear of the Lord is the instruction for wisdom, and before honor comes humility." True honor comes after humility.

I love to watch great athletes, but I love it even more when they don't appear to realize their greatness. I've always felt that way about one of my favorite running backs, Herschel Walker. He and I attended the University of Georgia together, along with about 29,998 other people. We did meet once, but I doubt he remembers me, unless the little guy who waited on him in a parking lot late one night comes back to his memory. I love the fact that he is one of the greatest running backs to play college and pro football, but he was never really the topic of his own conversations. Herschel is a humble guy and not real

> "**Pride moves us to bow down before the mirror rather than before God.**"
>
> John Ortberg

impressed with himself. That is an equation for true honor.

We should always remember that anything good in us is God in us. We can boast in Jesus, but other than who God is in us, we really don't bring anything to the table. If you really want to score points in life, you must start with humility. Consider the message of Proverbs 22:4: "The reward of humility and the fear of the Lord are riches, honor, and life." The riches that come from humility may be financial, but they may come in other forms such as a blessed family, a secure job, and a life of joy. Notice that this proverb connects humility with *the fear of the Lord.* Humility without Christ may lead to admiration by others and some meaningful blessings in this life, but when you at the fear of the Lord, your blessings extend into eternity.

Making a Mid-course Correction

Proverbs 26:12 leads us to know that pride only bears rotten fruit: "Do you see a man wise in his own eyes? There is more hope for a fool than for him." Are you wise in your own eyes but a fool in the eyes of the Lord? What are you going to do about your conclusions? Do you find that you are your favorite topic of conversation? Do you hold people captive with your long discourses and not care about their thoughts or opinions? If so, then you need a mid-course correction. Somewhere along the way, you have gotten out of line.

The reality is that it is easy to get out of line. We are kind of like the vehicles we drive. Imagine buzzing along the road at 45 miles per hour, and you hit a pot hole. Unfortunately, you will probably need a front-end alignment on your car. If you choose not to visit the tire store for the adjustment, you will eventually ruin your tires. Life is full of pot holes. It may have come in the form of an abusive parent or demeaning friends. You may have struggled in school or felt like a failure in sports. A lot of things can come along the way that may cause us to work extra hard to build up our own esteem. We have forgotten that we are special in the eyes of the Lord. We find ourselves talking more and more about our greatness and everyone else's weaknesses. We become *wise in our own eyes*. If you don't get a realignment, you're going to be broken down on the side of the road.

Proverbs 30:32 tells us the first step for a realignment: "If you have been foolish in exalting yourself or if you have plotted evil, put your hand on your mouth." What is God saying through this verse? Be quiet! Quit talking about yourself and about your greatness and knowledge. Spend time listening and focusing on other people. Maybe your first words should be, "I'm sorry." Start with saying those two important words to God with a repentant spirit. Proverbs 21:4 says, "Haughty eyes and a proud heart, the lamp of the wicked, is sin." Repentance opens the door for a fresh start.

When you talk to others, maybe you should ask questions instead of give answers. Give credit to others instead of taking credit for yourself. I once heard John Maxwell say, "It's amazing what we can accomplish if we don't care who gets the credit."

When we begin to focus on other people and get our eyes off of ourselves, the transformation of our character will be amazing. We will find deeper friendships and strengthened marriages. We will see the accomplishments of others and enjoy the smiles of people in our presence. Proverbs 19:6 states, "Many will seek the favor of a generous man, and every man is a friend to him who gives gifts." Think about the application of this truth when it comes to being generous with our attention to others. Think about the beauty of giving the gift that builds other people up. Imagine the transformation of your home if you put on humility in place of pride. It's never too late for an alignment.

FURTHER THOUGHT

- Why do you think God hates pride?

- What are some things that are an abomination to you? What do you think are some of the consequences of someone with a proud heart?

- Does it bother you that God wants us to worship Him? Make a list of benefits you experience when you worship. Is it possible that God knows that the only way you will truly be blessed is to surrender to His sovereign rule as your King? Since God is sovereign, doesn't He deserve your allegiance?

- How does pride bring destruction to a person's life?
- Make a list of reasons for why you are not "all that." What are some steps you can take to put on a life of humility?
- Do you find that you are the favorite topic of your conversations? Do you need to put your hand over your mouth? What steps will you take to set aside pride?

CHAPTER TWENTY-FOUR
Living by Faith

I have heard people say that life can turn on a dime. This year, we have experienced that reality, so we no longer think of that statement as a quaint saying but an absolute truth. My wife, Sandra, has struggled with breathing issues and allergies for a number of years, so it was not too surprising to me when she began having a little trouble breathing this past January. The only unusual thing was that January is not normally a season when she struggles with allergies, but then again, Georgia weather is quite unpredictable.

When I returned from a ministry trip to Mexico in early February, Sandra's condition had worsened a little, and she told me that she was going to let our daughter, who is a physician's assistant, listen to her lungs. She was concerned that she might get pneumonia. After her examination, our daughter felt like everything sounded okay, but she insisted that Sandra get an x-ray just to make sure.

On Tuesday morning of the next week, Sandra went to the doctor and came back by my office after the visit. We had talked about taking one of the cars to the shop, and I had thought about going to lunch together. She calmly told me about her visit with the doctor.

"My lungs are clear," Sandra reported, "and my breathing is better. All of my vitals were perfect, except they found a mass between my lungs."

My world stopped for a moment as hers had done a little earlier at the doctor's office. When a doctor says the word *mass*, that doesn't ever seem to be a good diagnosis. I know that mass usually means tumor, which is typically followed by surgery and chemotherapy and radiation and…who knows?

I don't usually jump to negative conclusions without facts that lead me down that path. The doctor mentioned the possibility of lymphoma but wanted her to come back for more tests that afternoon. She ended up having a tumor in the center of her chest that had grown into the sack around her heart. It wasn't lymphoma, and in the end, it wasn't cancer, though it could have been fatal. Two surgeries later, she is tumor free and far healthier than I am. We rejoice in our positive outcome, and I am still learning valuable life lessons from our experience.

Life Lessons in God's Forever Classroom

The first lesson was about the goodness of God. We experienced the goodness and provision of God through every step of our journey. It started by being accepted to the Cancer Treatment Centers of America within ten minutes of our initial diagnosis that afternoon. This wonderful organization has a hospital in our home town. Secondly, we had one of the finest thoracic surgeons in the country, and we were bathed in prayer from our friends and family night and day.

As we continued to experience God's miraculous power and love throughout our ordeal, I was reminded by many people about the goodness of God. The truth Pastor Bill Johnson wrote about in a book I had read a few months earlier became even more real in my heart: "We cannot exaggerate God's goodness. We can twist it, pervert it, dilute it, and misrepresent it. But the one thing we cannot do is exaggerate the goodness of God."[36]

As I sat in Sandra's hospital room after her first surgery, knowing that she still had the tumor, and we would have to go through surgery again, I pondered God's goodness. Two of my friends popped into my mind who had lost their wives in the past six months. Was God good to them? What if Sandra had more tumors and what if cancer had

> "The Lord is good to all, and His mercies are over all His works."
>
> Psalm 145:9

spread throughout her body leading to her eventual death? Would I still think that God is good?

I reflected upon the fact that nearly a year earlier I had planned my preaching for the upcoming twelve months, and I was currently preaching a sermon series entitled *Hope of the World*. I smiled as I thought about God's timing. That sermon series was for me. Even though the focus of the series was on the fact that God has called His church to share Christ's hope in the world, we have to experience hope through Christ first before we can be the hope the world needs.

I decided that if Sandra died with cancer, I would still trust God. God is good whether or not my news is good. I determined that my bad circumstances could not reduce God's character. I thought of my two friends who are now widowers. Is death so bad? I really didn't think Sandra's sickness would lead to death at this time, but if it did, is that so bad for a believer? If you want to live for eternity, odds are you're going to have to go through the door of death to get there. Unless Jesus returns during your life-time, there is a 100% chance that you're going to die at some point.

Before I closed my eyes in sleep that night, I lay there listening to my bride as she slept the sleep of faith. She trusted God completely. Proverbs 3:5-6 came to my mind. I mentioned this verse in the first chapter, which I had written before we knew that a life-threatening tumor was growing near the heart of my precious wife:

> *Trust in the Lord with all your heart*
> *And do not lean on your own understanding.*
> *In all your ways acknowledge Him,*
> *And He will make your paths straight.*
> —Proverbs 3:5-6

While drifting off to sleep, I mumbled a prayer: *I choose to trust because You are always good.* One lesson I reaffirmed

The Basis of Trust

How do we know that God is good and worthy of our trust? Let's face it. There are not many things we can trust in this world. We can't trust our home or Internet security because someone will figure out a way to breach it. We can't trust the government because our government is run by flawed human beings. In fact, everything and everyone around us is flawed, so we can't trust our doctors, our friends, our pastors, or even ourselves.

My last sentence sounds really cynical because we do find people in our lives who are trustworthy, but we know that sometimes people let us down because of either limited knowledge or spiritual or emotional weakness. However, the person who chooses not to trust anyone lives a lonely life. When someone hurts us or lets us down, we hopefully forgive them and restore our trust in them. Is there anyone in our lives who is 100% completely trustworthy?

God is not flawed by sin, and He is not weakened by emotional instability. He doesn't struggle with misunderstandings, and He won't cave to personal temptations. God is 100% worthy of our total and complete trust. Proverbs 16:20 states, "He who gives attention to the Word will find good and blessed is he who trusts in the Lord."

The Hebrew word *sakal* can be translated as *to understand*, *to study*, or *to be attentive*. It insinuates not just the discipline of personal study but also the result of full comprehension. The NASV translators chose to render *sakal* as *give attention*. This term can't just point to a casual reading of the Scripture. Giving attention to the Word of God is more than just a quick quiet time in the morning or a half-hearted attempt to listen to the sermon on Sundays. It means focusing our mind's attention and our heart's affection on the life-giving truth of God's inerrant, inspired Word. Solomon's conclusion was based upon the portion of Scripture he had available at the time. We have so much more now. If we give laser beam focus to God's Word, we *will* find good.

> "Turn to my reproof. Behold, I will pour out my spirit on you; I will make my words known to you."
>
> Proverbs 1:23

What does it mean to find good? It means that we will find truth and direction for our lives. By pouring through the pages of Scripture, we will discover guidance, counsel, teaching, and help. Paul told young Timothy about the benefits of God's inspired Word in 2 Timothy 3:16-17, "All Scripture is inspired by God and profitable for teaching, for reproof, for correction, for training in righteousness; so that the man of God may be adequate, equipped for every good work."

God's Word will never steer you down the wrong road. Holy Scripture becomes the standard by which we should measure every other statement, experience, and opinion. It is always 100% accurate, 100% helpful, and 100% true. We should never interpret Scripture by our experiences but rather interpret our experiences by Scripture. We will always find good in the Bible.

The second half of Proverbs 16:20 takes me back to life lesson number two I held to throughout our bout with needles, doctors, and hospital food: *blessed is he who trusts in the Lord.* I wrote about the wonderful word *blessed* in an earlier chapter. It simply means happy or full of joy. It carries with it the concepts of contentment, confidence, peace, and fulfillment. If we want this quality in our lives, we need to connect the first half of the couplet to the second. When we study and listen to and hold onto the Word of God, we will trust in the Lord. We will place bold confidence in the unwavering care and provision of our Heavenly Father. We will lean on Him when we don't understand something, and we will go to Him when we're knocked down by yet another catastrophe in this temporary experience we call life.

Giving close attention to the Bible and holding onto its truths inevitably leads to trusting in the Lord. You will either trust in the Lord or let go of the Scripture. If you hold onto God's Word, in time, you will discover that it is totally true and worthy of your trust. While other documents and people will let you down, God's Word is a breathed-out expression from God's Spirit. It can't be wrong! If you think it's inaccurate, it is only because your point of view is skewed. Keep reading and keep searching. You will not only find truth and accuracy of God's Word applied to your situation, but also you will find God in your circumstance. The result is BLESSING! Blessing includes the peace of God which passes all understanding (Philippians 4:7) and joy unspeakable and full of glory (1 Peter 1:8).

You Are Not Beyond God's Focus

Proverbs 22:19 is written to you: "So that your trust may be in the Lord, I have taught you today, even you." This scripture is fitting for a concluding thought on the book of Proverbs. I hope that as you have read through *Wisdom Speaks* that you have not only heard my voice but also the voice of the Lord. His Word is alive, and His Spirit is actively revealing truth. I trust that God has taught you today.

I love how God ended that verse with the two words *even you*. Have you ever felt like you were outside of God's notice? I assume that most of us know that God is aware of everything and everyone, but sometimes, we just feel insignificant in the universal gaze of our Creator. It's like somewhere in our twisted thinking, we process the fact that God was fully aware when someone like Billy Graham, Martin Luther King, or Mother Teresa had a thought or a need, but maybe we're not as high on His holy list of priorities. Wrong! That thought is from the pit. God gave us, *even you*, this wonderful book, called the

Bible, and He is constantly teaching us, *even you*, about its life-giving truths.

God is constantly teaching you about His truth so that your trust may always be in the Lord. Other things and other people may fail you, but God will never let you down. You may feel as if you dwell in the darkness of isolation, but even there, you will find your loving Father. Just keep reading, keep searching, and keep trusting. God will show Himself faithful.

From a dark hospital room to an empty board room, people have struggled with trust. This life is filled with events and circumstances that can destroy our faith, if we let them. But if we choose to hold onto God, we will find that He is first holding onto us. Even when we struggle with our circumstances, and even if we turn our backs on God, He will never leave us or forsake us. He waits patiently on us to return to His compassionate arms. He will help us sort through our situation and find hope. He will tenderly whisper in our ears that we were not made for this world but rather for the next.

> **"But the Lord is faithful, and He will strengthen and protect you from the evil one."**
>
> 2 Thessalonians 3:3

God's wisdom really does speak. Sometimes it shouts in the streets in the middle of the day, and sometimes, it whispers in the stillness of the night. Are you listening?

Further Thought

- Have you ever had a faith-challenging experience that tested your beliefs and called you to trust? What lessons did you learn? Is God still using it to teach you today?

- Have you ever questioned the goodness of God? What are your conclusions now? How can God be good when so many things around us seem bad?

- What are some of the consequences of leaning on your own understanding? How should you acknowledge God in all of your ways?

- Do you give attention to the Word of God? Real attention? What are some steps you can take to improve your focus on the Bible in the future?

- Write down a list of blessings that you have experienced in your life.

- Have you ever felt like God has overlooked you? How does it make you feel when you read that God has included *even you*?

A Word from the Author

Thank you so much for reading *Wisdom Speaks*. I hope that you enjoyed it and that you found encouragement through your study of God's Word. God gave us Proverbs as a guide for living, but through every book of the Bible, we will find that the first Guide we need is a person: Jesus Christ. If you've never considered the claims of Christianity, I hope you will read the next section on How to Become a Christian.

I would enjoy hearing from you, so I'm including my social media contact information below. Feel free to share your thoughts about the book or any of my other books. I would also enjoy having the privilege to pray for you, so please pass along any prayer requests you have on your heart.

If you have enjoyed *Wisdom Speaks*, I'd be grateful if you would take a few minutes and leave a review on Amazon. May God bless you on your journey to know Him and to serve Him.

Tim Riordan

Personal Website and Blog: timriordan.me
Facebook Author Page: facebook.com/authortimriordan
Twitter: www.twitter.com/tim_riordan
You can also find me on Goodreads.

HOW TO BECOME A CHRISTIAN

The book of Psalms is often read as a source of comfort and encouragement. It is important that we all understand that comfort and encouragement begins with a relationship with Jesus Christ. This appendix is provided to help you enter into a personal relationship with the One Who loves you and died so you can obtain eternal comfort and lasting security. If asked, many people in the United States would claim to be Christians, but what does it really mean to be a Christian? How does one "cross over" to a life of faith?

We must first understand a few truths. One critical thing we need to know is that God made us for relationships, and the number one relationship He made us for is the relationship with Himself.  While God wants a relationship with us, the fact is that deep down in our hearts, we long for a relationship with God. Sometimes we try to fill that longing with all manner of things such as careers, accomplishments, financial success, patriotism, sex, hedonism... The list could go on and on. In all of our attempts to fill the void in our lives, we simply come up empty-handed, or maybe I should say "empty-hearted." Earlier in this book, I referred to Pascal's quote: "There is a God-shaped vacuum in the heart of every man." If we try to fill the void in our lives with anything other than God, the void will remain just that–a void. Our longing, or our hunger, is for God and God alone.

The Bible teaches that every human being is born separated from God because of sin. Romans 3:23 says, *"For all have sinned and fall short of the glory of God."* A few verses prior to this, the Bible says, *"There is none righteous, not even one"* (Romans 3:10). Our society has tried to hide the reality of sin, but the fact is sin is not only all around us, but it is also all in us.

Sin could be defined as missing the mark of God's perfection. It is doing, saying, or thinking anything contrary to the ways and will of God. We are all guilty. We can try to redefine the term or compare ourselves to people of lesser morals, but the bottom line is that every human being is born with a nature to do wrong, and we also occasionally, or not so occasionally, chose to sin. One problem we have is that while we are not righteous, God IS righteous and holy. He can have nothing to do with sin, even though He loves the sinner (see Romans 5:8). This creates a great divide between us and God. The natural result of humanity apart from God is death. Romans 6:23

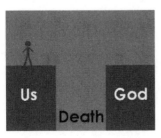 says, *"The wages of sin is death…"* This concept of death is more than just ceasing to have a heartbeat and a brain wave. This "death" means eternal separation from God.

People try to get to God through all manner of means. Most people think that if they are good enough, God will give them a pass into heaven. It is almost as if there is a large scale in heaven where all of our deeds are weighed. The good deeds are placed on the plate to the right and the bad deeds are placed on the left. If the good deeds outweigh the bad deeds, then we feel as if God is obligated to let us in to His heaven. The Bible says in Isaiah 64:6 "*all our righteous deeds are like a filthy garment*," and Ephesians 2:8-9 clearly says we are not saved by doing good works: "*For by grace you have been saved through faith; and that not of yourselves, it is the gift of God; not as a result of works, so that no one may boast.*"

While God is compassionate, merciful, and gracious, He is also holy, righteous and just. If God simply gave us a pass and let us into His heaven, He would not be righteous and just. If He just sent us all to hell with no hope for eternal life, He would not be gracious. God's answer, and our solution, is Jesus Christ. God sent His Son to die for the sins of the world. John 3:16 says, "*For God so loved the world, that He gave His only begotten Son, that whoever believes in Him shall not perish, but have eternal life.*" Jesus paid for our sins with His own life and then rose again from the dead declaring He is indeed God (see Romans 1:4).

God has given to us an option: either we pay for our sins through our own eternal death and separation from God, or we allow Christ's death to pay for our sins as we trust Him as our Savior. In essence, Jesus became our bridge to the Father. Through Jesus Christ, and only through Jesus Christ, we can enter into a relationship with our Creator. Jesus said, "*I am the way, and the truth, and the* 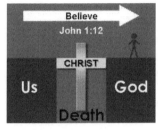 *life; no one comes to the Father but through Me.*" Acts 4:12 says of Jesus, "*And there is salvation in no one else; for there is no other name under heaven that has been given among men by which we must be saved.*"

We enter into a relationship with God through repentance of our sin and faith in Jesus Christ. Repentance means turning around. Whereas, once we were following our own way and our own desires, to repent means we turn and follow God's way and seek to fulfill His desires. Placing our faith in Jesus means more than just intellectually accepting the facts about Christ's identity and work. The Bible says in James 2:19: "*You believe that there is one God. Good! Even the demons believe that—and shudder*" (NIV). True faith comes as we surrender our lives to Jesus Christ allowing Him to be the King of our heart and the Leader of our life. Romans 10:9-10 says, "*If you confess with your mouth Jesus as Lord, and believe in your heart that God raised Him from the dead, you will be saved; for with the heart a person believes, resulting in righteousness, and with the mouth he confesses, resulting in salvation.*"

Christianity is a choice to surrender to Jesus Christ as the Lord of your life. Surrender means totally giving your life into the hands of someone else. Imagine drowning in a lake, and a lifeguard swims out to rescue you. The only way you can be saved from sure death is to quit fighting and surrender to the saving grasp of the lifeguard. Becoming a Christian is not just praying a prayer. It is not just going to church. It is not just trying to reform your life. Becoming a Christian is turning from sin and self and choosing to follow Jesus as your Sovereign King.

You can express this decision in a prayer as you cry out to God. If you have never done this and would like to, why not bow your head right now and tell Jesus that you acknowledge you are a sinner in need of forgiveness. Tell Him you believe that He died for you and rose again and ask Him to forgive you for your sin and come into your life. Commit yourself to be a Christ-follower for the rest of your days. Thank Him for His grace and pledge yourself to begin your new life today by seeking to grow as a new believer. I encourage you to do this right now. The Bible says in 2 Corinthians 6:2, "*Behold, now is the acceptable time; behold, now is the day of salvation.*"

What's next? While going to church doesn't save you, it sure helps you grow as a Christian. You will build relationships with other Christians who are seeking to grow in Christ and serve God with their lives. You will be encouraged in your faith and will grow in your understanding of the Bible, God's Word. I encourage you to find a Bible-believing church to attend where the Bible is taught and good Christian friendships can be enjoyed.

Is there someone who would like to hear of your decision to become a Christian? Why not call them right now and let them know of your new faith? Do you have Christian friends whom you admire? Why not call them right now and ask if you can go to church with them on Sunday? If you do not have Christian friends with whom you can share your decision, simply tell someone close to you. If you already attend a Bible-believing, Bible-teaching church, give your pastor a call, and let him know of your decision to trust Christ as your Savior.

Welcome to the Family of God!

Special thanks to Heather Bible Chapel (http://heatherbiblechapel.org) for assistance with "The Bridge" graphics.

NOTES

Chapter One

1. Max Anders, "Proverbs," *Holman Old Testament Commentary, vol 13*, (Nashville, B&H Publishing Group, 2005),14.

Chapter Two

2. Tremper Longman, *How to Read Proverbs*, (Downers Grove, Illinois, Intervarsity Press), 16.

Chapter Three

3. "Cost of National Security," *National Priorities Project*, March 19, 2018, https://www.nationalpriorities.org/cost-of (accessed on April 18, 2018).

Chapter Seven

4. Laura Entis, "Chronic Lonliness Is A Modern-day Epidemic," *Fortune*, June 22, 2016, http://fortune.com/2016/06/22/loneliness-is-a-modern-day-epidemic (Accessed on May 5, 2018).
5. Michael Bader, "How Can We Stop America's Deadly Epidemic of Lonliness," *Films for Action*, March 6, 2018, https://www.filmsforaction.org/articles/how-can-we-stop-americas-deadly-epidemic-of-loneliness (accessed on March 18, 2018).
6. Larry Crabb, Forewarad to *The Connecting Church: Beyond Small Groups to Authentic Community* by Randy Frazee, (Grand Rapids, Zondervan Publishing House, 2001, 13.
7. Theological Wordbook of the Old Testament #698 p. 305
8. "Disabled Group Conquers Mount Rainier, Ice and all," *New York Times*, archives 1981, accessed on March 3, 2018, https://www.nytimes.com/1981/07/04/

us/disabled-group-conquers-mount-rainier-ice-and-all.html (accessed on January 14, 2018).

Chapter Eight

9. Rick Warren, "God's Purpose in Suffering," *Daily Hope*, May 21, 2014, http://pastorrick.com/devotional/ english/ god%27s-purpose-in-suffering, (accessed on March 22, 2018).

Chapter Nine

10. "The Laziest Countries in the World," *The Daily Beast*, February 15, 2010, https://www.thedailybeast.com/the-laziest-countries-in-the-world (accessed on November 16, 2017).

11. Emin Dinlersoz, "Business Formation Statistics: A New Census Bureau Product that Takes the Pulse of Early-Stage U.S. Business Activity," *United States Census Bureau*, February 8, 2018, https://www.census.gov/ newsroom/blogs/research-matters/2018/02/bfs.html (accessed on February 15, 2018).

12. "Overweight and Obesity Statistics," *National Institute of Diabetes and Digestive, and Kidney Diseases*, https://www.niddk.nih.gov/health-information/health-statistics/overweight-obesity (accessed on March 2, 2018).

13. "Notable Quotes from Billy Graham," *Billy Graham Evangelistic Association*, November 5, 2009, https://billygraham.org/story/notable-quotes-from-billy-graham/ (accessed on February 1, 2018).

Chapter Eleven

14. W. Maynard Pittendreigh, "The Mark of Discipleship – Generosity," October 26, 2013, http://www.graceful sermons.com/ 2013/10 (accessed on February 8, 2018).

15. Andrew Greely, "America's Disease is Greed," *The Chicago Sun Times*, August 20, 2004,

https://www.commondreams.org/views04/0820-09.htm (accessed on February 10, 2018).

16. Duane A. Garrett, *Proverbs, Ecclesiastes, Song of Songs*, vol. 14, The New American Commentary (Nashville: Broadman & Holman Publishers, 1993), 172.

Chapter Thirteen

17. Alexandria Hein, "QLaser Infomercial Doc Gets 12 Years In Prison for Selling Scam Device," *Fox* News, April 24, 2018, http://www.foxnews.com/health/2018/04/24/qlaser-tv-infomercial-doc-gets-12-years-in-prison-for-selling-scam-device.html (accessed on April 24, 2018).

Chapter Fourteen

18. John MacArthur, "The Only Way to Happiness: The Beatitudes," p.129

19. D. Martin Lloyd Jones, "Studies in the Sermon on the Mount"

20. Jenny Santi, "The Secret to Happiness is Helping Others," *Time Magazine*, August 4, 2017, http://time.com/4070299/secret-to-happiness/ (accessed on March 3, 2018).

Chapter Fifteen

21. Mary Elizabeth Dallas, "Road Rage Rampant In America," *WebMD*,https://www.webmd.com/mental-health/news/ 20160714/road-rage-rampant-in-america, (accessed on 5/7/2018.

22. "Abortion Statistics," *American Life League*, updated March 26, 2015, https://www.all.org/learn/abortion/abortion-statistics/ (accessed on 5/9/2018).

Chapter Sixteen

23. Gina Bellefante, "Facebook, Generator of Envy and Dread," *The New York Times*, April 13, 2018, https://www.nytimes.com/2018/04/13/nyregion/facebook-generator-of-envy-and-dread.html (accessed on 4/17/18).

24. Francis Brown, Samuel Rolles Driver, and Charles Augustus Briggs, Enhanced Brown-Driver-Briggs Hebrew and English Lexicon (Oxford: Clarendon Press, 1977), 888.

Chapter Seventeen

25. Abigail Geiger, "8 Facts about Love and Marriage in America," *Pew Research*, http://www.pewresearch.org/fact-tank/2018/02/13/8-facts-about-love-and-marriage (accessed on March 19, 2018).

26. "U.S. Divorce Statistics," Divorce Magazine, July 13, 2015. http://www.divorcemag.com/articles/us-divorce-statistics (accessed on March 8, 2018).

27. Avery Foley, 'Sexual Immorality Increasingly Acceptable—Unless It's Adultery," *Answers in Genesis*, May 27, 2017, https://answersingenesis.org/morality/sexual-immorality-increasingly-acceptable-unless-adultery (accessed on March 21, 2018).

Chapter Eighteen

28. Ken Ham, "Survey: 81% of Americans See 'Declining Morality' in the US," May 2, 2017, https://answersingenesis.org/blogs/ken-ham/2017/05/02/survey-81-americans-see-declining-morality-us (accessed on March 23, 2018).

Chapter Nineteen

29. "Fast Facts," *Teen Health and the Media*, https://depts.washington.edu/thmedia/view.cgi?section=medialiteracy&page=fastfacts (accessed on April 5, 2018)

30. P.J. O'Rourke, *Brainy Quote*, https://www.brainyquote.com/quotes/p_j_orourke_124820?src=t_parenting (accessed on April 2, 2018).

Chapter Twenty

31. "What Does the Bible Say about Slander," Got
    Questions Ministries, https://www.gotquestions.org/
    Bible-slander.html (accessed May 14, 2018).

Chapter Twenty-one

32. Patty Ann Malley, "Pinocchio Awards: Who's the
    Biggest Liar of them All," *WND*,
    http://www.wnd.com/2018/04/pinocchio-awards-
    whos-the-biggest-liar-of-them-
    all/#XfVI1GJl1ycV6ELh.99 (accessed on May 15,
    2018).

33. Dan Bobinski, "The Ripple Effect of Workplasce
    Lies," *Management.Issues*, http://www.management-
    issues.com/opinion/6600/the-ripple-effects-of-
    workplace-lies (accessed on May 15, 2018).

Chapter Twenty-two

34. Newt Gingrich, "Brainy Quotes," https://www.
    brainyquote.com/quotes/newt_gingrich_107062?src=t
    _hard_work (accessed on May 15, 2018).

Chapter Twenty-three

35. Martin H. Manser, "The Westminster Collection of
    Christian Quotations," Westminster John Knox Press,
    Louisville, KY, 2001, 299.

Chapter Twenty-four

36. Bill Johnson, *God is Good: He's Better Than You Think*,
    Destiny Image Publishers, Shippensburg, PA, 2016, 35.

BOOKS FROM GREENTREE PUBLISHERS

Immovable: Standing Firm in the Last Days

By Tim Riordan

Does Bible prophecy indicate that we are living in the last days? What should Christians do to be ready for the days ahead? Dr. Tim Riordan shares biblical truths on Bible prophecy and how the Church can stand firm in the last days. This book also offers a small group discussion guide.

Songs from the Heart: Meeting with God in the Psalms

By Tim Riordan

Songs from the Heart: Meeting with God in the Psalms is a Bible study/devotional on one of the most loved books of the Bible: the Psalms. Join Dr. Tim Riordan as he shares insights on these beloved passages through Bible teaching and storytelling, making personal application to your life.

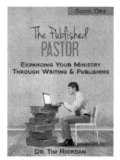
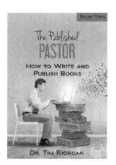

The Published Pastor: Books One & Two –
Expanding Your Ministry Through Writing and Publishing & *How to Write and Publish Books*
By Tim Riordan

Would you like to expand your ministry by turning your next sermon series into a book your congregation can pass on to others? *The Published Pastor* series is a collection of books that will encourage you to write and offer you the step-by-step help you may need to become a published author.

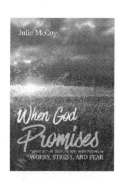

When God Promises
Taking God at His Word will free you from Worry, Stress, & Fear
By Julie McCoy

This six-week study draws on the experiences of people in the Bible who discovered the power of taking God at His word. As you explore their stories you will learn how trusting God's faithfulness to do what He says will give you victory over worry, stress and fear.

The Long Way Home
By Judah Knight

Dive into an adventure of scuba diving, treasure hunting, danger and suspense in Judah Knight's exciting novel, The Long Way Home. When Meg was stranded in the Caribbean, her life was dramatically changed through an encounter with an old friend that turned into adventure, danger, discovery, and love. Enjoy flinch-free fiction that is safe for the whole family.

Consider other books in the Davenport Series

Book 5 scheduled for release in the summer of 2018.

Reaching for Life

By Victoria Teague with Connie J. Singleton

Following an eleven-year cocaine addiction and a dangerous career as a dancer in Atlanta's sex industry, Victoria Teague experienced what can only be called a miraculous rescue. For ten years after she left the clubs, she sat respectably in the pews of her church with a grateful heart and a zip-locked mouth. She built an entirely new life on top of embarrassing secrets from her past, and only a precious, trusted few knew her spiritual rags-to-riches story. That is until one ordinary day when she was asked to do anything *but* the ordinary. On that day, she was called not only to share her secrets, but also to spotlight them. To use them as her "street cred" to minister to other women in the strip clubs who desperately need a lifeline like the one she was offered. To seek the lost and give them hope for a better life.

For more information on any of our publications, visit www.greentreepublishers.com.

96429806R00148

Made in the USA
Columbia, SC
30 May 2018